SIR KNOWS BEST!

There's no stopping Fergie as Man United land their ninth Premiership crown...

YOU SELL YOUR NO.1 STRIKER. You then lose your new first-choice, one of your other main hit-men is injured, another shows a lack of form and for a handful of games you bring in a forward with no Premiership experience.

A recipe for disaster? Not if you are a canny Scotsman by the name of Sir Alex Ferguson.

Dutch striker Ruud van Nistelrooy upset the gaffer so he was sold to Real Madrid despite averaging more than a goal a game over the past five years for The Red Devils.

Fans questioned the reasoning behind that, especially with no replacement brought into Old Trafford.

And with Louis Saha proving injury prone and their favourite son Wayne Rooney hitting a barren spell in front of the sticks, the signs were ominous, despite United heading the title race.

They should know better than doubt Fergie! The call went out for Henrik Larsson. A hero at Celtic, a star at Barcelona, but then plying his trade back in his home country at Helsingborg. Surely, at the age of 35, his chance of a swansong in England's top-flight had now gone?

Wrong again! You can't keep a good man down – that's Fergie *and* Henrik – and although he only played in 13 games during his loan, the Sweden superstar proved that wherever he plays he scores with six vital goals.

He set United up for the title and the team responded, despite also having to play without dedicated skipper and right-back Gary Neville for many games.

They were just too good for Chelsea and ended the West Londoners' quest to make it three titles in a row.

FINAL COUNTDOWN

		P	W	D	L	F	A	GD	PTS
1	Man United	38	28	5	5	83	27	+56	89
2	Chelsea	38	24	11	3	64	24	+40	83
3	Liverpool	38	20	8	10	57	27	+30	68
4	Arsenal	38	19	11	8	63	35	+28	68

PREMIERSHIP FACT BOX 2006-07

- **TOP SCORER** Cristiano Ronaldo, 17.
- **HIGHEST CROWD** 76,098, v Blackburn.
- **LOWEST CROWD** 75,115 v Fulham.
- **CLEAN SHEETS** 16.
- **BLANKS** 4.
- **DOUBLE ACHIEVED** 12 (Wigan, Aston Villa, Watford, Tottenham, Charlton, Fulham, Liverpool, Bolton, Blackburn, Sheffield United, Everton, Man City).
- **DOUBLES SUFFERED** 2 (Arsenal, West Ham).
- **KEY WIN** 1-0 win at Liverpool.
- **WORST RESULT** 1-0 home defeat to Arsenal.
- **HAT-TRICKS** Wayne Rooney at Bolton.
- **NUMBER OF GOALSCORERS** 17.
- **PLAYERS USED** 25.
- **BAD LAD:** Paul Scholes, one red, eight yellows.

COMPLIMENTS OF THE SEASON

Who won what in 2006-07

SUNDERLAND

CHAMPIONSHIP CHAMPIONS

The Black Cats looked like they were heading for a second successive relegation until former Man United and Republic of Ireland midfield destroyer Roy Keane took over as boss. He made big changes on the pitch and the Wearsiders clinched the title ahead of Birmingham on the final day of the season, thanks to a stunning 5-0 win at relegated Luton.

SCUNTHORPE UNITED

LEAGUE ONE CHAMPIONS

Billy Sharp set a new club record of 32-goals in a season – which has stood for 45 years - as The Irons returned to the second-tier of English football for only the second time in their 97-year history. Nigel Adkins, who started the season as the club's physio, took over as boss and led them to the title ahead of Bristol City with three games to spare.

WALSALL

LEAGUE TWO CHAMPIONS

Relegated the previous season in rock bottom position, The Saddlers bounced back at the first attempt under new boss Richard Money. He had to admit to missing the goal that clinched Walsall's second title in 47 years (Division Four champions, 1960) – because he spent the last 20 minutes of the match in the players' tunnel!

CELTIC

SCOTTISH PREMIER LEAGUE, SCOTTISH CUP

The Bhoys retained the title with a staggering 12-point gap over Rangers. And boss Gordon Strachan saw his side completed a Double thanks to a 1-0 victory over Dunfermline in the Scottish Cup Final through an 84th-minute goal from Jean-Joel Perrier Doumbe. That made it four trophies from a possible six during Strachan's first two years in charge – and a place in the final 16 of the Champions League for the first time-ever!

DAGENHAM
CONFERENCE CHAMPIONS

Formed by a merger of clubs in 1992, a year after first entering the Conference, Dagenham and Redbridge appeared in the first-ever play-offs from this division and promised so much only to fade away. But under boss John Still they earned promotion to the Football League, despite having sold two of their best players.

CHELSEA
THE FA CUP

Chelsea's second cup final victory of the season was the first FA Cup Final at the new Wembley, where they took on champions Man United. The Blues won the trophy thanks to the only goal of the game, a late extra-time strike from Didier Drogba – but it's unlikely there will be a much duller game at the stadium!

CHELSEA
THE CARLING CUP

Theo Walcott fired The Gunners into a 12th-minute lead but Didier Drogba came to Chelsea's rescue with goals in the 20th and 84th minutes. But the game will forever be remembered for John Terry getting knocked unconscious by a boot in the face from Abou Diaby and the sendings-off in the 90th minute of John Obi Mikel, Kolo Toure and Emmanuel Adebayor.

HIBERNIAN
CIS CUP

John Collins became the first Hibbees boss in 16 years to lift a trophy thanks to the crushing 5-1 victory over Kilmarnock. Their last silverware had come in the same competition in 1991.

DONCASTER
JOHNSTONE'S PAINTS TROPHY

Bristol Rovers didn't concede a goal on the way to the final but were two down within five minutes against Doncaster. They levelled to reach extra-time but Graeme Lee's header won the trophy.

STEVENAGE
THE FA TROPHY

Ronnie Henry will go down in history as the first captain to lift a trophy at the new Wembley Stadium after Stevenage Borough's amazing comeback against Kidderminster. Boro were two down at half-time but hit three in the second-half in front of 53,000, the winner coming in the last two minutes from Steve Morison.

TRURO CITY
THE FA VASE

THE FA CARLSBERG VASE
WINNERS 2007

A goal down to AFC Totton after 28 minutes, Truro got the game to 1-1 by half-time then came back with two more strikes in the second 45 minutes. Nearly 28,000 saw a Cornish team earn victory for the first time.

SEVILLA
UEFA CUP

The all-Spain clash between Espanyol and Sevilla was 1-1 after normal time and 2-2 at the end of extra-time. But Sevilla retained the trophy for a second year with a 3-1 penalty shoot-out victory with former West Ham and Spurs striker Fredi Kanoute on the scoresheet.

AC MILAN
CHAMPIONS LEAGUE

AC Milan gained revenge over Liverpool for their incredible defeat in this competition's final just two years earlier. Then, the Merseysiders appeared dead and buried at 3-0 down after 45 minutes but stormed back to level the scores and earn a penalty shoot-out win. This time Milan, semi-final conquerors of Man United, scored a goal in each half from Filippo Inzaghi which meant Dirk Kuyt's last-minute strike was merely a consolation.

CRISTIANO RONALDO
FOOTBALL WRITERS', PFA PLAYER AND YOUNG PLAYER OF THE YEAR

The young Portugal winger expected a tough year from fans following his part in the sending off of Man United team-mate Wayne Rooney when their two countries clashed at the World Cup finals. Instead, he turned on the style and trickery to elevate himself into superstardom, picked up the top two awards from his fellow pros and bagged a Premiership winner's medal!

10 THINGS YOU SHOULD KNOW ABOUT...

CRISTIANO RONALDO

1 Cristiano was born on the small Portuguese island of Madeira, on February 5, 1985. He started playing football aged just three!

2 His full name is Cristiano Ronaldo dos Santos Aveiro. The "Ronaldo" bit came from his Dad's favourite actor, Ronald Reagan, who also just happened to be President of the United States!

3 His nicknames are Ronnie, Ron, Rocket Ronaldo, CR7 and Buzzed. Although opposition fans have called him worse!

4 Whilst playing for Sporting Lisbon in Portugal, then-Liverpool manager Gerard Houllier showed an interest in signing the flying winger but decided against the move because he was too skinny!

5 Man United came knocking after he gave Gary Neville a torrid time in a friendly and he arrived at Old Trafford for £12.24m in August 2003. At that time, the deal made him the most expensive teenage signing in Britain ever.

6 Sir Alex Ferguson says Cristiano – the first Portuguese star ever to play for United - is "the best young talent I have ever seen." He went some way to proving it by winning the Sir Matt Busby Player of the Year award following his first season with The Red Devils.

7 The person he would most like to meet is former boxing champion Mike Tyson (oh dear!) but his favourite actress is Angelina Jolie (hurrah!)

8 He helped take tournament hosts Portugal to the final of Euro 2004 but a shock defeat by Greece saw him leave the field crying like a baby!

9 Another shocker, this time at the 2006 World Cup. Loads of people – including Steven Gerrard who branded him "a disgrace" – blamed Cristiano for getting Wayne Rooney sent off in the quarter-finals. His hassling of the referee after Wazza's foul and then wink to his team-mates *was* a bit naughty, but they are still the best of mates!

10 Now one of the most brilliant players in the Premiership, Cristiano has confirmed that he sees his future at United, despite links with Spanish giants Barcelona and Real Madrid. He says: "I have always said that I would like to play in Spain one day, but not yet! If things keep going well I want to stay here at Old Trafford. I'm only thinking about Manchester United. I want to leave my mark on this era, win titles and be a figure in the history of this club."

FUNNY OLD GAME

A LOOK AT THE WACKY WORLD OF FOOTBALL...

Reading's new boy proved his fitness

Stuart Pearce practices his new dancing moves

Politicians always struggle to juggle the ball...

Ouch! Now that really does hurt!

Mini-Fowler gets ready to replace Dad Robbie

Michael Owen wondered why Big Sam was wearing a sash

A police web caught the dodgy new signing

Whose hair are you calling dodgy?

What was wrong with calling him a big girl?

13

Ronnie is spot-on

We're not quite sure about The Reebok knees up either!

Sheva explains how to play golf to model Jodie Kidd. She told him later how he's meant to put the ball in the net...

James Milner and Andy Van Der Meyde take up WWE

You nose that's disgusting!

Thierry was well impressed with Robben's diving

Oops - the ref was flagging a little...

Captain Blade reckons his Sheffield United side was a victim of relegation pirates...

Ronnie found the Manchester rain well cold

Bellamy's invisible golf club led to him getting a new Hammer...

THE ONES TO WATCH

We reveal some of the youngsters expected to make a BIG name for themselves over the next few years!

CRAIG CATHCART Manchester United

BORN: February 6, 1989, Belfast, Northern Ireland
POSITION: Defender **HEIGHT:** 6ft 2in **WEIGHT:** 11st 6lb

A tall, strong and composed centre-back, Craig is gradually breaking through the youth and reserve teams at Old Trafford. Has captained the Under-18s and represented Northern Ireland at youth level. Strong in the air and hard in the tackle, Craig is able to bring the ball out of defence and pick out a telling pass. Made the first-team bench towards the end of last season as The Red Devils faced a defensive injury crisis.

GRANT BASEY, Charlton Athletic

BORN: November 30, 1988, Farnborough
POSITION: Left-back
HEIGHT: 6ft 2in **WEIGHT:** 14st

A powerful left-back, Grant made tremendous strides in the latter half of his first full season as a scholar in 2005-06. Last campaign he was a regular in the reserves and will be looking to make the step up to first-team level as Charlton bid for promotion to the Premiership. Grant is a free-kick specialist and scored seven set-piece goals last term. Has also been selected for the Wales Under-21 squad.

SIMON COX, Reading

BORN: April 28, 1987, Reading
POSITION: Striker **HEIGHT:** 5ft 11in **WEIGHT:** 11st

Simon spent time on loan at Brentford and Northampton last season and impressed. Has been at Reading since he was nine years-old and can play in midfield as well as up front and scored numerous times for The Royal's reserves last season. Simon suffered a broken leg in September 2006 whilst on loan with Brentford but recovered sufficiently to return to action with the London club two months later. He was recently offered a new contract by Reading boss Steve Coppell as Northampton Town showed an interest in signing him on a permanent deal.

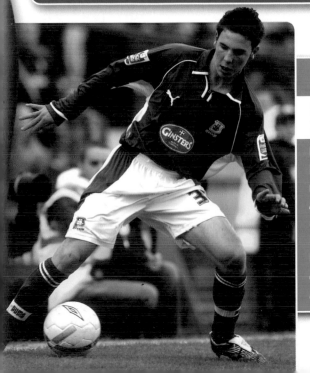

DAN GOSLING, Plymouth Argyle

BORN: February 2, 1990, Brixham, Devon
POSITION: Midfielder **HEIGHT:** 5ft 10in **WEIGHT:** 11st 2lb

Dan is still only 17-years-old but has already made an impression on the Plymouth first-team. The young midfielder can either play through the middle or on the right and was in fine form for Ian Holloway's side against Watford in last season's FA Cup quarter-final. Dan was a Manchester United fan as a boy and models his game on former Red Devils' legend Roy Keane. He spent a week training with Chelsea last season and if he continues to progress he will be in the thoughts of many Premiership managers. This season Dan will be looking to add to the 12 first-team appearances he made last term.

LIAM BRIDCUTT, Chelsea

BORN: August 5, 1989, Reading **POSITION:** Midfielder **HEIGHT:** 5ft 7in **WEIGHT:** 11st

The tough-tackling central midfielder is a product of Chelsea's academy and impressed in The Blues' youth side last season. Liam was also given his first taste of reserve team football after coming on as a substitute for the club's second string. The Berkshire-born youngster may be looking for a spell out on loan in future seasons to gain first-team experience, but next year he'll be chasing a place in Chelsea's reserve set-up.

KERREA GILBERT, Arsenal

BORN: February 28, 1987, Hammersmith, London **POSITION:** Right-back **HEIGHT:** 5ft 9in **WEIGHT:** 11st 1lb

The 20-year-old Arsenal defender is ready for regular first-team football after an impressive loan spell with Championship side Cardiff City last season. Kerrea has made a number of appearances for The Gunners, including one outing in the Champions League. He will have to battle two other young right-backs, Justin Hoyte and Emmanuel Eboue, for a start as he bids to secure his future at The Emirates. Has the potential to be one of Arsene Wenger's most talented young stars.

MICHAEL COULSON, Barnsley

BORN: April 4, 1988, Scarborough **POSITION:** Striker **HEIGHT:** 5ft 10in **WEIGHT:** 10st

The highly rated youngster signed for Barnsley in the summer of 2006 from Scarborough. He had been a revelation at Boro after making his first-team bow at the age of 16 and scored the equaliser for Barnsley against Southend United in the FA Cup last season. The 19 year-old centre-forward will be hoping to add to his goal tally and establish himself as a regular starter this season, especially after last year's top scorer Daniel Nardiello joined QPR in the summer.

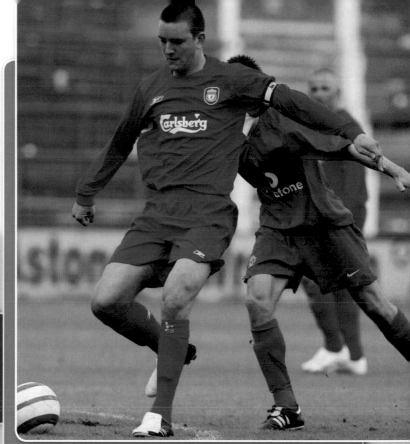

JACK HOBBS Liverpool

BORN: August 18, 1988, Portsmouth **POSITION:** Defender **HEIGHT:** 6ft 3in **WEIGHT:** 13st 4lb

The promising centre-back arrived at Anfield in the summer of 2005 from Lincoln City after impressing Rafa Benitez during a trial. Jack was part of last season's victorious Youth Cup-winning team and has also captained the reserves. He will be keen to make his first-team debut this season as he has been given a squad number. Can also play as a holding midfielder.

ADAM McGURK, Aston Villa

BORN: January 24, 1989, Larne, Northern Ireland **POSITION:** Striker **HEIGHT:** 6ft **WEIGHT:** 12st 1lb.

The promising hit-man could be the latest forward on the Villa books to graduate to the first-team after Luke Moore and Gabby Agbonlahor in recent seasons. The Northern Ireland-born youngster has represented his country at Under-16 and Under-17 level and broke into the Villan's reserve side last season.

KNOW YOUR FOOTBALL?

Check out just how smart you are by solving our puzzles and footie questions

10 QUESTIONS ON... THE CHAMPIONS LEAGUE FINAL

1. Who scored both goals for AC Milan when they beat Liverpool 2-1 in Athens in 2007?
2. **Name the only French club to have won the Champions League (in 1993).**
3. Who was the manager of FC Porto when they defeated Monaco 3-0 in the 2004 final?
4. **Which two Spanish clubs became the first-ever representatives from one country to both get to the final (in 2000)?**
5. Name the Arsenal player who was sent-off in the 2006 final against Barcelona in Paris?

6. **Which English ground hosted the 2003 final between AC Milan and Juventus?**
7. Who was in goal for Liverpool when they dramatically beat AC Milan on penalties in 2005?
8. **Name the scorer of Manchester United's first goal when they came from behind to beat Bayern Munich in injury time in 1999.**

9. Which team has lost three Champions League Finals since 1997?
10. **In which Russian city will the 2008 final be played?**

GUESS WHO?

Can you identify the six players in these pictures?

TRUE OR FALSE

Can you separate fact from fiction?

1. Chelsea have won the FA Cup the most number of times.
2. **Rafa Benitez used to play in goal for Barcelona in Spain.**
3. David Beckham once went on loan to Preston North End.
4. **Carlos Tevez has won an Olympic Gold medal with Argentina.**
5. Peter Crouch was a youth team player at Tottenham.

THE EYES HAVE IT

Look into their eyes and see if you can identify these six England players?

1

2

3

4

5

6

ANAGRAMS

The five names below are actually anagrams of current players or managers. With the help of our clues, see if you can identify them:

1. BRIGADIER ODD
Nothing strange about his goal in the FA Cup final.

2. DION INFRA RED
The word "red" is a distinct clue here.

3. BERNARD TEN
North London fans will be hoping for more than ten goals

from this striker in 2007-08.

4. MAJOR LINT
Very astute manager who signed "Bernard Ten" above.

5. JODY SHANNON
A bit of a girls name maybe, but don't whisper that to this Everton hot shot.

Hidden in the grid is the name of an English Championship club who have previously won the UEFA Cup. Answer the questions below then re-arrange the letters in the grid to fill in the name.

IN THE BOX

Box 1: Which team won the UEFA Cup in 2007?
Sevilla (W)
Barcelona (F)
Newcastle United (K)

Box 2: For which club does former England captain David Beckham play?
Real Madrid (U)
Man United (D)
L A Galaxy (I)

Box 3: Which one of these people has never managed England?
Glenn Hoddle (B)
Terry Venables (A)
Alan Curbishley (W)

Box 4: Who plays at the San Siro stadium?
Benfica (I)
Inter Milan (S)
Derby County (G)

Box 5: Which of these England players did not play at the 2006 World Cup?
Gary Neville (E)
Jamie Carragher (A)
Shaun Wright-Phillips (H)

Box 6: Which Scottish club are known as the "Jam Tarts"?
Celtic (C)
Dundee United (S)
Hearts (P)

Box 7: Who is the president of FIFA?
Sepp Blatter (O)
Sven Goran Eriksson (L)
Zinedine Zidane (N)

Box 8: Which two colours do you traditionally associate with Stoke City?
Yellow and green (D)
Red and white (I)
Claret and blue (S)

Box 9: How many Premiership goals did Didier Drogba score last season?
15 (D)
20 (C)
32 (O)

Box 10: In which country do Boavista play?
Turkey (L)
Croatia (R)
Portugal (T)

Box 11: Who has won the most FA Cups out of these three clubs?
Aston Villa (N)
Blackburn Rovers (R)
Chelsea (O)

1	2	3	4	5	6	7	8	9	10	11

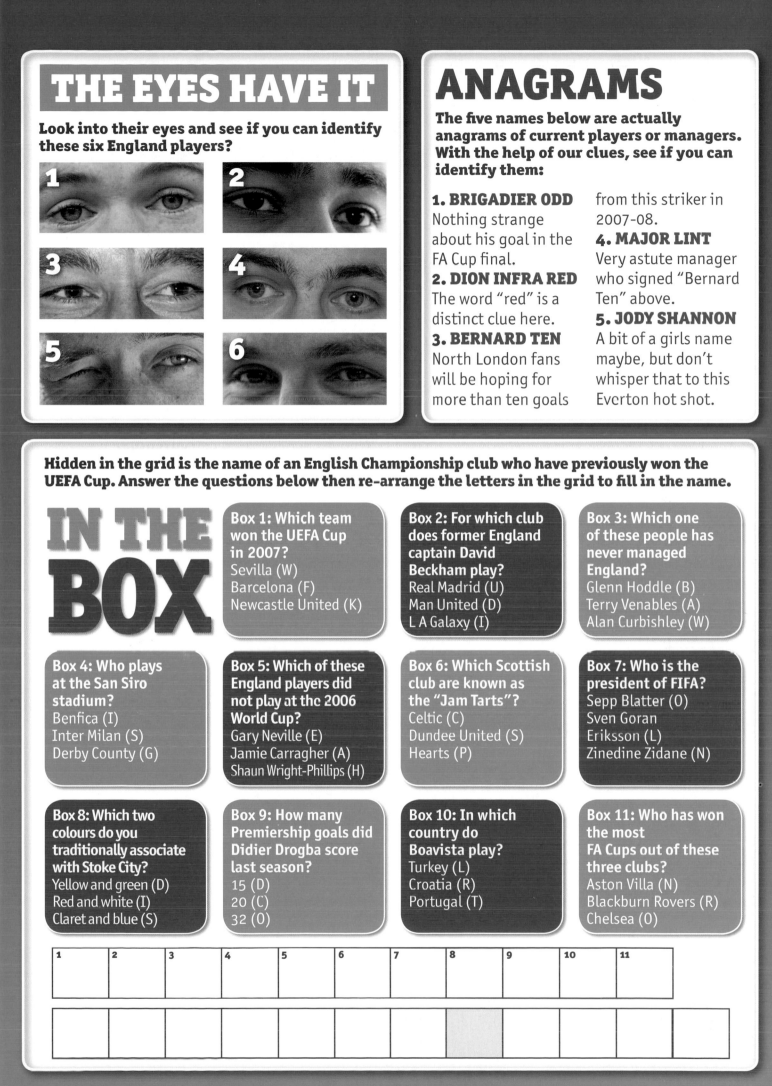

A-Z

CURRENT PREMIERSHIP IMPORTS

...the top foreign players currently plying their trade in England's top-flight!

A **NICOLAS ANELKA**
The France striker made his name at Arsenal in the late 1990s before a £23m move to Spanish giants Real Madrid. Anelka suffered a frustrating spell at the Bernabeu, despite getting his hands on the Champions League in 2000. Moves to Paris Saint Germain, Manchester City and Fenerbahce, and a spell on loan at Liverpool followed, before Big Sam Allardyce signed him for Bolton last season. A clinical finisher, Anelka always provides a goal-scoring threat and can be world-class at times.

B **DIMITAR BERBATOV**
The silkily skilled Bulgaria striker made a very impressive start to his career in England. Spurs beat a number of top European clubs, including Man United, to sign him at the start of last season when they paid Bayer Leverkusen £10.9m for his services. They were rewarded with a whole host of top-class performances and goals.

C TIM CAHILL

The Everton midfielder provides a real goal-scoring threat with his direct style of play and ability to arrive late in the box. Impressed for Australia in the 2006 World Cup finals and has provided excellent value for money for the Toffee's since his £2m move from Millwall in 2004.

D DIDIER DROGBA

Chelsea's best player last season, Drogba has become one of the most feared centre forwards in Europe. The Ivory Coast striker has improved each season since his £24m move from Marseille in 2004. He has cut down on the theatrical diving and concentrated on his game and The Blues are clearly reaping the rewards.

E MICHAEL ESSIEN

Chelsea's Ghana midfielder simply eats up the ground playing either as a defender or midfielder. Essien's energy levels are amazing and his performances for The Blues since his £26m move from Lyon in 2005 have ensured he's one of the first names on Jose Mourinho's team sheet. His rare goals tend to be spectacular.

F CESC FABREGAS

It's easy to forget that Arsenal's young Spain midfielder is still only 19 as he plays with a composure beyond his years. Fabregas was the youngest player to ever take to the field for The Gunners when he was just 16 years and 177 days. He has already established himself in Spain's national side and looks set to become one of the world's best in years to come.

G GILBERTO SILVA

The Brazil World Cup-winner has proved to be another one of Arsene Wenger's transfer gems. Gilberto joined Arsenal following the 2002 World Cup for a bargain £4.5m and has been a vital part of their midfield ever since. Captained the side in Thierry Henry's absence last season and alongside Fabregas has formed a midfield partnership that has given experience, energy and solidity.

H TIM HOWARD

The USA keeper arrived in England when he was bought by Man United from MLS side Metro Stars in 2003 to replace Fabien Barthez. A loss of form and the arrival of Edwin van der Sar cost him the No.1 spot at Old Trafford. Tim went on loan to Everton who were so impressed that they took him permanently in January 2007 on a five-year deal.

I ANDREAS ISAKSSON

Man City signed Isaksson, a former Juventus player, in August 2006 from French side Rennes. The Swedish stopper hasn't quite made the desired impact at Eastlands yet, thanks to Nicky Weaver's impressive form last season, but there is no doubting his class. He has earned 44 caps for Sweden and had some impressive performances in the 2006 World Cup finals.

J JUSSI JAASKELAINEN

Quite simply one of the best keepers in the Premiership. On his day the Bolton No.1 can be unbeatable, using his agility and lightning quick reactions to keep the ball out of the net. The Finland international has been linked to bigger clubs on many occasions but says he will see out the last year of his contract at The Reebok before deciding on a move.

K — DIRK KUYT

A tireless worker for the Liverpool cause, Kuyt has become a firm favourite with the Anfield faithful since his £10m move from Feyenoord in summer 2006. The Holland striker perhaps doesn't score as many goals as he should but his selfless runs and eye for a cross or pass have created plenty of goals for his team-mates.

L — LOMANA LUA LUA

The former Newcastle man has impressed at Portsmouth under Harry Redknapp and has the ability to score spectacular goals, which are almost as good as the back-flip filled celebrations that follow them! The DR Congo striker has suffered several injury problems but when he's fit and on form few defenders relish playing against him.

M — STEED MALBRANQUE

The classy French midfielder looks as though he's been playing in the Tottenham midfield for years, having only arrived at White Hart Lane in summer 2006 from Fulham. Quick, direct and capable of providing a goal-scoring threat from either wing, Malbranque could be a vital factor in taking the North London club to the next level.

N — RYAN NELSEN

The New Zealander has been a rock at the back for Blackburn since his move from American club DC United in 2005. His strength, speed and ability to read the game have given the Ewood Park outfit a more solid backline. With a promising partnership forming with Christopher Samba at the centre of the Rover's defence, Mark Hughes' side shouldn't concede many this season.

O — OBAFEMI MARTINS

The lightning quick Nigeria striker made quite an impression in his first season at St James' Park. Still only 22 years of age and learning all the time, Martins has scored some spectacular goals and worked hard for the Newcastle cause, often having to play as a lone striker. His debut season was so impressive he was linked with moves to Man United, Arsenal and Chelsea.

P — MORTEN GAMST PEDERSEN

Blackburn's Norway winger has one of the sweetest left feet in the Premiership. He provides a massive threat from corners and free-kicks and can score spectacular long-range efforts. As he continues to add consistency to his game it surely won't be long before one of the big four attempt to lure him away.

Q — FRANCK QUEUDRUE

A no-nonsense French defender who also poses a threat in the opponent's area at set-plays. Had an impressive few years at Middlesbrough before then-Fulham boss Chris Coleman took him to Craven Cottage for an undisclosed fee in 2006.

R — CRISTIANO RONALDO

After an amazing season for Man United the young Portugal winger has established himself as one of the very best players in the world. Ronaldo has added an end product to all the tricks and flicks and propelled United to the title as he collected Player of the Year awards. Now the main man for Portugal too having taken over the great Luis Figo's mantle.

S LOUIS SAHA

Ever-improving France forward who has finally justified Sir Alex Ferguson's faith in him. When fit, he looks to be worth every penny of the £12.8m Manchester United paid Fulham for his services in 2004. Superb in the air, with excellent hold-up play and the ability to score with either foot, Saha provides the perfect foil for Wayne Rooney.

T KOLO TOURE

Vastly underrated central-defender who's reading of the game and organisational skills hold the Arsenal back line together. Capable of playing in every defensive position and in midfield, Toure is a manager's dream. The Ivory Coast star should be a cornerstone of The Gunner's defence for many years to come.

U ULISES DE LA CRUZ

The Ecuador international is currently on the books at Reading after previous spells at Aston Villa and Hibernian. The right-sided defender or midfielder is a star in his homeland but has never quite made the adjustment to Premiership football. Good going forward but occasionally suspect when defending.

V NEMANJA VIDIC

Vidic has been a monster at the back for Manchester United since he joined from Spartak Moscow for £7.2m in 2006. The Serbia defender has formed a great partnership with Rio Ferdinand and played a major part in United's recent renaissance. His positional play is top class and his ability in the air and strength in the tackle strike fear into the hearts of forwards. Vidic also grabs his fair share of goals.

W WILLIAM GALLAS

Signed for Arsenal from Chelsea as part of the deal that saw Ashley Cole arrive at Stamford Bridge. So far injuries have prevented the Frenchman showing his best form for The Gunners.

At Chelsea, Gallas was one of the best defenders in the Premiership and if he stays fit the versatile former Marseille man should form a solid partnership with Toure.

X XABI ALONSO

Alonso keeps The Reds ticking over in the middle of the park and is often a star performer in the Champions League. The Spain star is an ideal foil for Steven Gerrard, and can also weigh in with some vital goals of his own. Famed for his long range shooting, which has included two goals scored from inside his own half in recent seasons!

Y YAKUBU AIYEGBENI

The Yak goes from strength-to-strength with each season he plays in the Premier League. After an impressive spell with Portsmouth the powerful Nigeria striker moved in 2005 to Middlesbrough for £7.5m, but has been linked to bigger clubs. Not always been first choice for Boro whose fans would like to see him increase his work rate – but you can't argue with his goal record.

Z DIDIER ZOKORA

Another Ivory Coast international, Zokora was quietly impressive at Tottenham during his first season in English football. Spurs signed him for £8m from St. Etienne to beat off interest from Man United, who had been keeping tabs on the defensive midfielder. Strong in the tackle and composed on the ball, Zokora should make the holding role at White Hart Lane his own.

A-Z

ALL-TIME PREMIERSHIP IMPORTS

There's been some cracking foreign players in the Premiership since it kicked-off for the first time in 1992. Here are just a few stars...

A **ANDREI KANCHELSKIS**
The flying Ukraine winger who played a major part in much of Manchester United's success of the early 1990s. Almost exclusively right-footed, Kanchelskis gave United great balance on the right-wing, with a young Ryan Giggs operating down the opposite flank. He scored his fair share of goals too, and was always a threat on the counter attack. Left Old Trafford in 1995 to join Everton.

B **DENNIS BERGKAMP**
One of the best foreigners to have played in the Premiership. The Dutchman showed sublime skill and scored vital goals during his 11-year spell with Arsenal. Taken to North London by Bruce Rioch in a £7m deal from Inter Milan in 1995, Bergkamp will go down as one of the best signings Arsenal ever made.

ERIC CANTONA

The catalyst for Manchester United's dominance of English football in the 1990s and one of the most popular players to have ever worn the red shirt. Cantona is a United legend and his skill, arrogance and goal-scoring ability transformed The Red Devils from Premiership challengers to champions. Retired at the peak of his powers in 1997 aged just 30 and moved into acting.

PAOLO DI CANIO

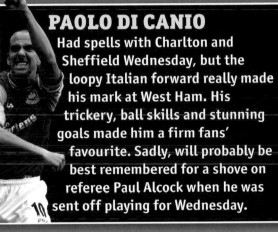

Had spells with Charlton and Sheffield Wednesday, but the loopy Italian forward really made his mark at West Ham. His trickery, ball skills and stunning goals made him a firm fans' favourite. Sadly, will probably be best remembered for a shove on referee Paul Alcock when he was sent off playing for Wednesday.

EMERSON

Perm-haired Brazil midfielder who never really fulfilled his potential in the Premiership. Joined Middlesbrough in 1996 from Porto and along with fellow Samba star Juninho brought some quality to Teesside. Scored some spectacular goals but soon moved on to Tenerife.

FREDI KANOUTE

The former West Ham and Spurs striker was sold to Sevilla in 2005 for almost £5m after he went missing from a pre-season tour. The Mali hit-man has lifted the UEFA Cup for the past two seasons with his new club, which has resulted in reports that the speedy frontman could return to England.

DAVID GINOLA

Flowing-haired Frenchman who starred for Newcastle and Spurs in the mid to late 1990s. Ginola was an extravagant and creative winger with an eye for the spectacular. Also had rather less successful spells with Everton and Aston Villa. Despite his lack of hard work or tracking back to defend, most supporters would agree that thanks to his entertainment value, the star of those shampoo adverts was worth it!

JIMMY FLOYD HASSELBAINK

One of the best foreign strikers to grace the Premiership, Jimmy has scored goals wherever he's played. George Graham brought the Dutchman to England in 1997 when he signed him for Leeds. After a successful spell with Atletico Madrid, Hasselbaink went on to score goals for Chelsea, Middlesbrough and Charlton.

ILIE DUMITRESCU

Clever Romanian midfielder who had a brief spell with Tottenham in the early 1990s. Dumitrescu was part of an exciting Spurs side that also included his fellow countryman Georgiou Popescu, German striker Jurgen Klinsmann and England's own Teddy Sheringham. Never really adapted to the English game but showed glimpses of his class.

JUNINHO

A hero for thousands of Middlesbrough fans during his three spells at The Riverside, the diminutive Brazilian captured the imagination and stole the hearts of the Teesside faithful. He terrorised English defences in his first spell, but struggled to make the same impact upon his return in 2002, although he was involved when Boro won their first major trophy, the League Cup in 2004. A 2002 World Cup winner.

K JURGEN KLINSMANN

The first major European star to ply his trade in the Premier Leauge, striker Klinsmann signed for Spurs in 1994. The composed German immediately made his mark with a debut goal against Sheffield Wednesday which he cheekily celebrated with a dive! Klinsmann left Spurs a year later but retuned for a second spell at White Hart Lane in 1997 to save Tottenham when they were struggling at the wrong end of the table.

L ANDERS LIMPAR

The Sweden winger made his name at Arsenal, who he joined just before the start of the Premiership. Lifted the FA Cup following a move to Everton, where he later fell out of favour.

Sold in January 1997 to Birmingham, but made just four appearances for the St. Andrews side before returning to his homeland.

M GAIZKA MENDIETA

The former Spain midfielder provided a major coup when he was first taken on loan before being signed by Middlesbrough from Lazio in 2004. Was part of the side that won Boro's first silverware – the League Cup – and although he has been an influence, injuries and a lack of fitness saw his time at The Riverside end on a low.

N PETER NDLOVU

Speedy Zimbabwean forward who terrorised Premiership defences in the

early 1990s whilst in the sky blue of Coventry City. Ndlovu had the ability to beat his man and also score from a variety of different angles. One of the more entertaining foreigners to play in the Premier League in its formative years.

O JAY-JAY OKOCHA

The magical Nigerian midfielder possessed bucket loads of natural ability and an extremely powerful shot. He signed for Bolton Wanderers in 1998 and spent four seasons at the club. When Jay-Jay was in the mood he could control games with ease.

P ROBERT PIRES

Took a season to adjust to the pace of the Premiership, but once he did Pires emerged as one of the most dangerous midfielders in the competition's history. Operating on either flank, or through the middle for Arsenal, the Frenchman scored some vital goals and linked up superbly with Henry and Bergkamp. Won the league title in 2002 and 2004.

Q QUINTON FORTUNE

Versatile South African defender-midfielder whose true class was rarely on show due to terrible luck with injuries. Joined Man United in 1999 in a £2.5m deal from Atletico Madrid, and never let The Red Devils down during his seven-year spell at Old Trafford. Recently released by Bolton.

R BRIAN ROY

The skilful Dutchman formed a potent striking partnership with Stan Collymore at Nottingham Forest in the 1994-95 season. Signed in a £2.9m deal from Italian side Foggia, Roy went on to score 13 league goals in his first season for the East Midlands club. The speedy striker moved to Germany's Hertha Berlin for £1.5m in the summer of 1997.

S PETER SCHMEICHEL

The greatest keeper to ever play in the Premier League and probably one of the best there has ever been. The great Dane spent eight years with Manchester United, winning an amazing ten major trophies. Schmeichel also turned out for Man City and Aston Villa towards the end of his career.

W PAULO WANCHOPE

Elastic-legged Costa Rican who could be awesome or awful. Wanchope made his mark in England when he scored after a mazy run on his Derby debut against Man United at Old Trafford. The South American striker could never reach the level of consistency required to succeed in the Premiership and after spells with West Ham and Man City moved to Spain's Malaga in 2004.

T EMERSON THOME

Brazil-born centre-back who played for Sheffield Wednesday, Chelsea, Sunderland, Bolton, Derby and Wigan during his time in England. Strong in the air and good on the deck and could provide a threat in the penalty box from set pieces.

X ABEL XAVIER

Probably not one of the greatest foreigners to have played in England, but definitely worth a mention due to his dodgy Mr Whippy head barnet! The Portuguese defender can be a class act on his day and put in some solid performances for Everton, Liverpool and Middlesbrough before moving to LA Galaxy.

U UWE ROSLER

The German striker had an up and down career in England with Man City, but always worked tirelessly. Rosler scored 29 goals in 79 Premier League games for City, but could not stop them being relegated twice in three years. Also had brief spells with Southampton and West Brom and has recently managed in Norway.

Y YOURI DJORKAEFF

A World Cup and European Championship winner with France, the striker stunned football with a move to Bolton from Kaiserslautern in 2002. At the age of 34, he scored 20 goals in 75 games for The Trotters before leaving The Reebok to join local rivals Blackburn. He managed just three games at Ewood Park before departing to become the first Frenchman to play in America's MLS. Retired from the game with an ankle injury in 2006.

V PATRICK VIEIRA

The Senegal-born France midfielder was a star of the two great Arsenal teams that Arsene Wenger has created in the last ten years. Vieira formed an impressive partnership with Emmanuel Petit in the late 1990s and became the talisman, driving force and captain of "The Invincibles" of 2004.

Z GIANFRANCO ZOLA

One of the classiest players to have stepped on to a Premiership pitch, Zola came to England at the peak of his powers and showed his true class during his seven-year spell with Chelsea. The Italian's skill and vision makes him one of The Blues' all-time greats. Zola won the FA Cup twice and the Cup Winners Cup once whilst at the Bridge.

KAKA!

WHY ALL THE FUSS ABOUT THIS BLOKE?

Well he plays for Italian giants AC Milan and is probably just the best player in the world, that's all. Doh!

WHAT KIND OF NAME IS KAKA ANYWAY?

His real name is Ricardo Izeeson dos Santos Leite. "Kaka" came about because his brother couldn't pronounce his first name correctly when they were both kids. But it's a shame that the word kaka means poo in Spanish!

FROM THE SLUMS OF BRAZIL HE FOUND FAME AND FORTUNE. WHAT A STORY!

Well not quite. He was in fact born into an upper-middle class family and originally set his sights on becoming a professional tennis player. Very posh!

SO HE HAD IT EASY THEN...

Sorry. Wrong again. At the age of 18 he fractured his spine in a swimming pool accident and could have been paralysed. Whilst recuperating he set up a ten-point plan to get his career back on track. And he's ticked every one off his list!

WHAT CAME AFTER THE ACCIDENT?

Well having battled back to fitness he smashed his way into his club side's first-team, scoring 12 goals in 27 appearances during his debut season. A star was born...

DID YOU KNOW?
He was so skinny as a 17-year-old that he had to be put on a special "fattening-up" diet by his club!

KAKA'S TEN-POINT PLAN

1) Play again [after fracturing his back in a swimming pool accident]. ✔

2) Get taken on by Sao Paulo as a professional footballer. ✔

3) Get into Sao Paulo's senior squad of 25. ✔

4) Get into the squad of 18 involved in the games. ✔

5) Get into the team's starting 11. ✔

6) Play in the World Youth Cup for Brazil. ✔

7) Receive a call-up for the Brazilian senior squad. ✔

8) Play for Brazil. ✔

9) Play in the World Cup. ✔

10) Move to a major club in Italy or Spain. ✔

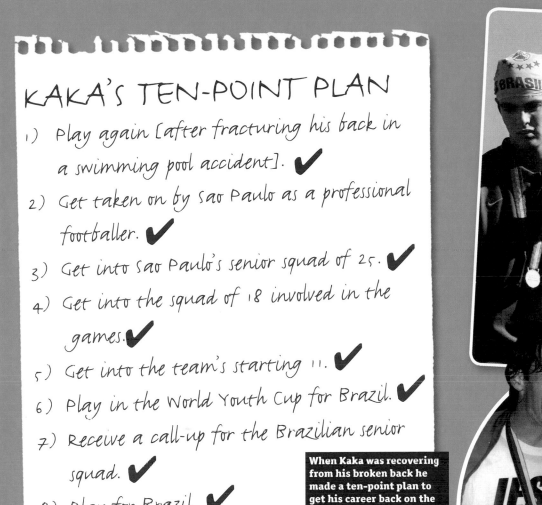

When Kaka was recovering from his broken back he made a ten-point plan to get his career back on the rails. This is what the note may have looked like...

DID YOU KNOW?
Kaka is a very religious guy. He even has the words "I Belong to Jesus" stitched into his adidas boots!

HE HAS A WORLD CUP WINNER'S MEDAL DOESN'T HE?
Yeah, Brazil won in 2002 although Kaka only played a few minutes as a sub. But his reputation was enough to see him snapped up by AC Milan for £6m. The Milan president later described the fee as "peanuts." He was dead right!

BECAUSE...?
Chelsea were rumoured to be interested in tabling a £50m offer just a few months ago (he's mates with Andriy Shevchenko). And currently he is seen as Brazil's most important player – even ahead of Ronaldinho!

IS THERE A BIT OF RIVALRY GOING ON THERE?
We don't think so. Kaka told us: "I have tried many times to get Ronaldinho to come and join us [at Milan]. I really enjoy playing with him. He is an amazing talent and I would give anything to play at club level with him."
Kaka and Ronaldinho in the same team? Watch out Europe!

KNOW YOUR FOOTBALL?

Are you a footie mastermind? Our great puzzles and super crossword will find out!

GETTING SHIRTY

Can you identify these ten international strips?

 **1**

 **2**

 **3**

 **4**

 **5**

 **6**

 **7**

 **8**

 **9**

 **10**

WHAT DO YOU KNOW ABOUT MICHAEL OWEN?

1. Which club did Michael support when he was a boy?
a. Newcastle
b. Liverpool
c. Everton

 **1**

2. How many goals did Michael score in Liverpool's 2001 FA Cup victory against Arsenal?
a. 1
b. 2
c. 3

3. What number shirt did Michael wear during his brief time at Real Madrid?
a. 7
b. 11
c. 14

 3

4. Against which country did

 **4**

his 2006 World Cup come to an end due to injury?
a. Portugal
b. Ecuador
c. Sweden

5. Name the manager who signed Michael for Newcastle.
a. Bobby Robson
b. Graeme Souness
c. Glenn Roeder

FOOTIE CROSSWORD

ACROSS

1 Nickname associated with the club from Gay Meadow (6)

4 - - - Carson, England Under-21 keeper who starred in Charlton's relegation battle last season (5)

9 Portugal and Chelsea defender, Ricardo - - - (8)

10 James - - -, winger who returned to Newcastle from a loan spell at Villa (6)

11 Old Trafford boss, Sir - - - Ferguson (4)

12 First name of Jamie Redknapp's father (5)

15 Ex-Arsenal, West Brom and Nigeria striker who helped Pompey up the table last season (4)

18 Kevin - - -, Bolton skipper who led his side to UEFA Cup qualification (5)

20 The Canaries, managed since last October by Peter Grant (7)

21 - - - Cisse, Marseille striker who was on loan there from Liverpool last term (7)

22 Club whose boss, Dario Gradi, retired after 24 years, in 2007 (5)

24 Liam Gallagher's Oasis brother - a celebrity Man City fan (4)

25 Ex-Feyenoord Ivorian forward, Salomon - - -, establishing himself at Chelsea (5)

28 The nickname of League Two play-off qualifiers, Lincoln City (4)

30 Spanish midfielder, Mikel - - -, a hero at Goodison (6)

31 Home ground of Macclesfield Town (4,4)

32 - - - Park, historic Dublin venue made Ireland's new home in 2007 (5)

33 Former England striker, - - - Cole, who helped with Birmingham City's promotion campaign last year whilst on loan from Pompey (6)

OLLY DAYS...

He's barking mad and we love him! Plymouth and former QPR boss Ian Holloway is king of the quotes... but don't ask us to explain some of the things he rants on about. We haven't a clue what he means either!

FIRE!
"I reckon the ball was travelling at 400mph, and I bet it burned the keeper's eyebrows off."

SNAKES ALIVE!
"It's like putting a snake in a bag, if you do not tie it up, it will wriggle free."

HEARTBEAT
"There was a spell in the second-half when I took my heart off my sleeve and put it in my mouth."

TURTLE POWER
"I mean no respect to Donatella. I'm sure she would not be flattered to hear she looks like Marc Bircham."

TXT WARNING...
"I think us human beings will end up with thumbs like giant crabs pretty soon because of all the texting that goes on and the playing of these stupid computer games. We'll have lost the art of talking."

BUM DEAL
"If anybody's offended by seeing a backside, get real. Maybe they're just jealous that he's [Joey Barton] got a real nice tight one, with no cellulite or anything."

...AND WE LOVE THE PLAYERS WHO GIVE US A LAUGH TOO!

"Dad talks like he played for Brazil - but I believe my Mam was very skillful for Woolworths."
John O'Shea, Republic of Ireland and Man United defender, goes shopping for compliments

"Al Pacino is my favourite actor and I always take my copy of *The Godfather* trilogy with me - I never get bored of those films. I often put one on safe in the knowledge that if I drop off it doesn't really matter because I already know the ending!"
Bolton captain **Kevin Nolan** is in the picture

"I wouldn't be bothered if we lost every match this year as long as we win the league."
Errr, can someone make a point to Australia and Newcastle striker **Mark Viduka?**

"It's been harder this year, Liverpool have got better, Manchester United have got better, Arsenal have got better, and Tottenham have joined the quartet of five teams."
Joe Cole, England and Chelsea midfielder, loses count...

35

THE TOP TEN
1. Range Rover Sport
2. BMW X5
3. Bentley Continental GT
4. Audi Q7
5. Aston Martin DB9
6. Mini Cooper S
7. Mercedes CLS
8. Audi TT
9. Chrysler 300C
10. Range Rover Vogue
(Kahn conversion)

• *Thanks to www.vehicleconsulting.com*

Newcastle striker Shola Ameobi with his Mercedes CLS

Watford defender Danny Shittu with the popular BMW X5

Rangers' Kevin Thomson plumps for the best-selling Range Rover Sport

EXCLUSIVE!

STARS AND THEIR CARS

BET YOU THINK star football players all drive top-of-the range sports cars and luxury Bentleys. Wrong!

Shoot arranged a special survey involving more than 100 players across a selection of clubs in England and Scotland, most of them in both countries' Premier Leagues.

And top of the pile by a long, long way is the Range Rover Sport – which is believed to have replaced the BMW X5 at the top of the list over the past 12 months.

Martin Thomas, from Oldham, who supplies a lot of cars to the stars, admits: "Probably most of the cars on here are pretty obvious and predictable but a couple of them, notably the Chrysler 300C and Mini Cooper S may come as a bit of a surprise.

"The Range Rover Sport has easily been the biggest seller, taking approximately 30 per cent of the cars sold."

Our list takes into account cars both bought and leased by players.

Who drives what?

CRAIG BELLAMY
West Ham
Ferrari F360

THIERRY HENRY
Barcelona
Porsche
911 Turbo

DAVID JAMES
Portsmouth
BMW M6

SCOTT PARKER
West Ham
Porsche
Cayenne

ROBBIE SAVAGE
Blackburn
Mercedes
SL65

THEO WALCOTT
Arsenal
Audi Q7

JOHN TERRY
Chelsea and
England
Range Rover
Sport 4.4

BANG!
Wales midfielder Robbie Savage celebrated his move from Crewe to Leicester City by blowing his signing on fee on a PINK Porsche. Just a few days later the car blew up!

MASCOT MADNESS!

Can you name which clubs these 12 mascots belong to?

1 MIGHTY MARINER

2 DEEPDALE DUCK

3 BEAU BRUMMIE

4 BAGGIE BIRD

5 H'ANGUS MONKEY

6 BILLY THE BADGER

9 MOONCHESTER

7 HERCULES LION

10 SKY BLUE SAM

8 BUMBLE BEE

11 ROAR LION

12 FRED THE RED

SMACK DOWN!

"I always have a good battle with John Terry. I've caught him a couple of times and gave him a bloody lip and he's caught me, but that's the way it is, just get up and get on with it." Bolton's iron man striker Kevin Davies comes up against Chelsea's superman defender

PREMIERSHIP SECRETS

Star players tell us what life is really like behind the scenes at their clubs!

NAILED!

"Jose Goncalves never trains unless he is fits. If he had a broken finger nail or a torn eyelash you would find him in the treatment room." Scotland keeper Craig Gordon pulls no punches about Hearts' Portugal left-back

OUT OF TUNE!

"Before every game we have someone's iPod on so it can be a variety of music. If it's crap the player responsible is hammered!" Striker David Bentley reveals that there can be disharmony in Blackburn's dressing room

BOSH!

"I'm always getting ticked off, even in training and it can be from my fellow players, not just the boss. But you just take these things on your chin as you are always learning." Defender Steven Taylor isn't really the bad boy of Newcastle – he just likes to get stuck in!

CLUCKING!

"I love chicken, if I could eat it every day I would." Striker Lomana Lua Lua ruffles a few feathers at Portsmouth

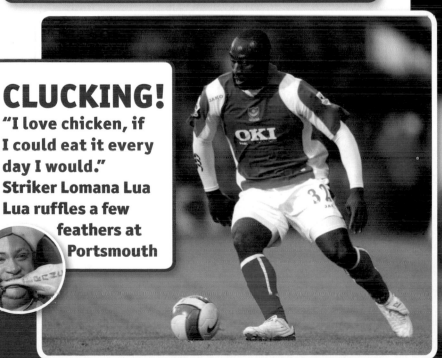

NAME DROPPER!

"I used to share a room with Edwin Van der Sar and carry water bottles for Thierry Henry." Defender Mortiz Volz has played at Fulham and Arsenal, so he knows famous people...

10 THINGS YOU SHOULD KNOW ABOUT...
JAMIE CARRAGHER

1 Jamie Lee Duncan Carragher is a Scouser through and through, having been born in Bootle, Merseyside on January 28, 1978. To this day he lives just five miles away from where he grew up and went to school.

2 He joined Liverpool as an apprentice and, alongside a certain Michael Owen, helped the club win the 1996 FA Youth Cup.

3 Having broken into the first-team in the late 1990s, Carra spent the first few years as a "utility" footballer - playing in central-defence, both full-back positions and midfield! He became Liverpool's first-choice centre-half when Rafa Benitez became boss.

4 Carra is the longest-serving player currently on Liverpool's books. And has just agreed a contract extension to 2009.

5 He was England Under-21 skipper and with Aston Villa's Gareth Barry set a record for the most appearances with 27 caps. That has since been beaten by keeper Scott Carson.

6 Many fans reckon he should play alongside John Terry in the heart of England's defence – his manager certainly does! "For me, he's one of the best in the country and I'd like to see him playing for England because he deserves it," says Rafa Benitez.

7 Carra featured in three games in the 2006 World Cup finals, starting against Sweden, and then as a substitute versus Ecuador and Portugal. In that last game in the quarter-finals, he scored with his first penalty in the shoot-out but was forced to retake it because the referee hadn't blown his whistle! He missed the second and England went out.

8 Just like fellow Anfield hero Robbie Fowler – released at the end of last season – he used to support big rivals Everton!

9 Carra was placed seventh in the all-time ranking of "100 Players Who Shook The Kop" which appeared on Liverpool FC's official website.

10 He does so much work for charity and helping local youngsters that he was awarded the freedom of his home borough of Sefton. Apparently this allows him to drive a herd of sheep through the streets of Bootle, if he so wishes! We think he'd much rather the sheep came with mint sauce!

IN PRAISE OF FERGIE

He's the most successful boss in the history of the Premiership and his achievements with Man United are never likely to be beaten. We get the lowdown on **SIR ALEX FERGUSON** from some of his rivals... and take a look at some of the great Scot's own views on football

WHAT THEY SAID ABOUT HIM...

"When people talk about modern-day managers it is my own belief that he is the greatest in the game."
Aston Villa boss Martin O'Neill

"For him to keep going is remarkable. He stands out with his will to win, he knows football, he knows his players and he knows his own club inside-out."
Former United captain Roy Keane

"You can't imagine life at United without him. One day it will happen, we are all aware of that. When it does it will be a great shame due to what he's achieved. It won't be soon, as he is still desperate to win trophies."
United midfielder Paul Scholes

"It wouldn't surprise me if he carried on for five to ten years. Why should he leave? He's as determined as ever. It's the continual challenge here that keeps him young."
Club captain Gary Neville

"When you think that the average life of a manager is one year and seven days, and somebody has done 20, it is a remarkable achievement. I feel we had some heated times – but time will settle things and there is a respect there now."
Arsenal manager Arsene Wenger

"I once rang him up and was on for ten minutes about players and he told me about every player, their strengths and their weaknesses. I put the phone down and I said 'I bet he even knows the Dunfermline groundsman'. So I rang him back and said 'Hey Alex, I forgot to ask you about the Dunfermline groundsman' and, by God, he did know his name and where he came from!"
Former Sheffield United boss Neil Warnock

"I believe that Sir Alex is number one in England and one of the top two or three in the world. I have found him a nice person, you can talk to him without any problems."
Liverpool's Rafael Benitez

"At the end of United's Treble-winning season in 1999, we were having a cup of tea at the training ground and he was already talking about what was needed for the season after. That's how he's been so successful!" **Steve McClaren, England manager and former United assistant boss**

"People did not know how much he used to watch the youth team when the likes of the Nevilles, Butt, Scholes and Beckham were in it, he knew every player well. Nobody at Old Trafford thought you could emulate Sir Matt Busby or beat his record. But Sir Alex did."
Former United youth coach Eric Harrison

WHAT HE'S SAID...

"I can still remember my very first game in charge away at Oxford. I had done my team-talk and was going into the dugout when I saw the bus driver sitting there. He was even giving the tea out at half-time. Let's say that quickly stopped."
On changing the culture at Old Trafford

"At the end of this game, the European Cup will be only six feet away from you and you'll not even be able to touch it if we lose. And for many of you that will be the closest you will ever get. Don't you dare come back in here without giving your all." **The half-time talk during the 1999 Champions League Final**

"I can't believe it. I can't believe it. Football... bloody hell."
His immediate reaction to the 1999 Champions League triumph

"What does he [Arsene Wenger] know about English football, coming from Japan?"
Fergie's first spat with Monsieur Wenger

"They say he's [Arsene Wenger] an intelligent man, right? Speaks five languages! I've got a 15-year-old boy from the Ivory Coast who speaks five languages!"
Another dig at the Arsenal coach

"I'm privileged to have followed Sir Matt [Busby] because all you have to do is to try and maintain the standards that he set so many years ago."
On bringing success back to Old Trafford

ALEX McLEISH

And it really is a case of hair yesterday and gone today for the Scotland boss. We're sure the Tartan Army can lend him one of those big ginger wigs they wear.

TONY MOWBRAY

This one will stitch up the West Brom boss! Just wait until his Baggies' players see the dyed hair and ask if he is still a medallion man under that shirt and tie.

TRADING

SAMMY LEE

He looked a bit puzzled as a Liverpool player... and not a lot has changed since he became Bolton manager! Well okay, the once flat hair now stands up on end!

ROY KEANE

Roy Keane reckons he's more cool, calm and collected as a manager. Really? We aren't fooled by that tie – the glare looks more frightening than his shouting!

LAWRIE SANCHEZ

Did Fulham's gaffer really wear lipstick? Sorry Lawrie, only joking! Mind you, we're not so sure about that barnet! Collar and tie suits you much better sir...

PAUL INCE

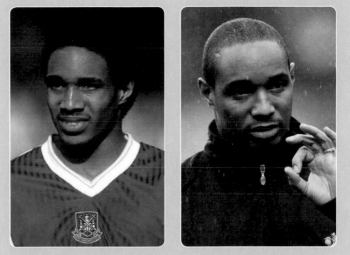

Paul Ince always reckoned he was The Guv'nor and looks a lot more like the gaffer in his more recent picture on the right. Oh, sorry, he *is* in charge now...

FACES

We've taken eight managers and players and transported them back to yesteryear. Ready, set, HAIR we go!

CHRIS HUTCHINGS

Everyone was asking who Chris Hutchings was when he took over as Wigan's new boss. You didn't recognise him as the former Chelsea player then?

MARTIN O'NEILL

Aston Villa boss Martin O'Neill reveals that he used to have a forest on his head as a player in Nottingham. He grew it to match the badge on his shirt!

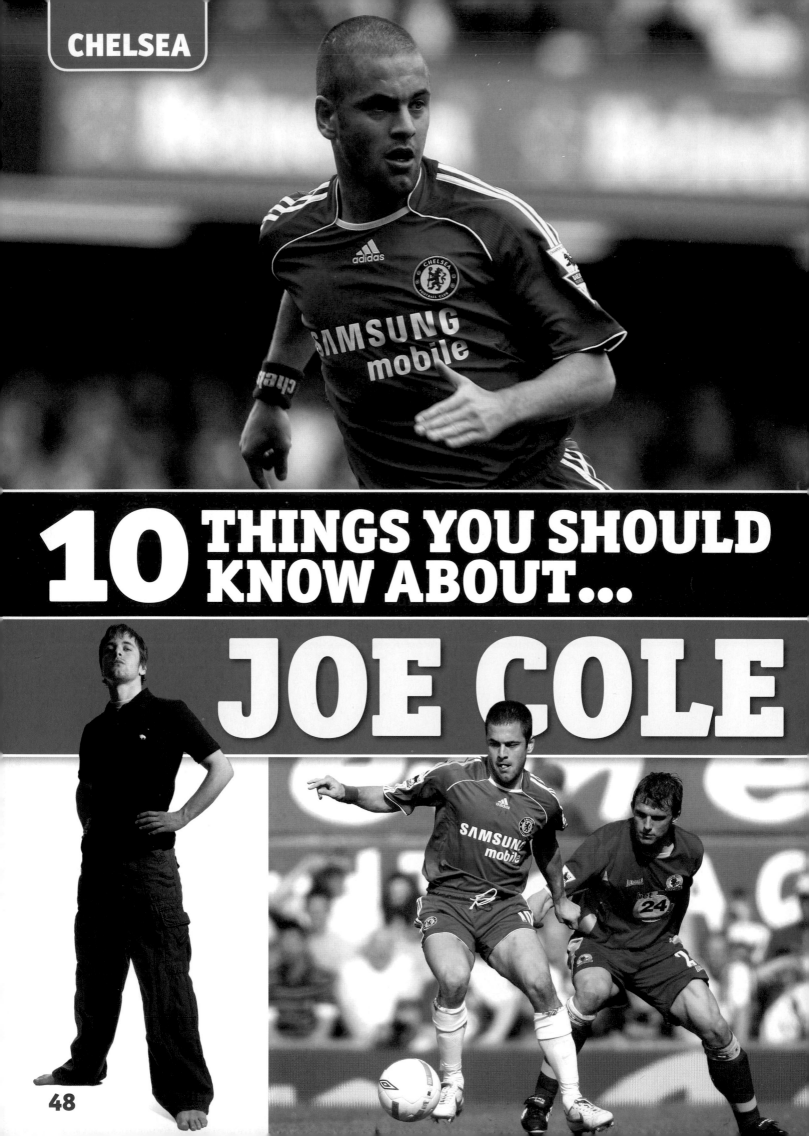

10 THINGS YOU SHOULD KNOW ABOUT...
JOE COLE

1 Joseph John Cole was born on November 8, 1981 in Paddington, London, before moving to the borough of Camden at the age of seven.

2 A product of West Ham United's amazing youth system, Joe made his first-team debut at the age of 17. He became Hammers' club captain just two years later!

3 Joe once selected the following legendary players to be in his all-time XI (with himself in midfield!): Peter Schmeichel, Cafu, Bobby Moore, Roberto Carlos, Luis Figo, Patrick Vieira, Diego Maradona, Roberto Baggio, Rivaldo and Ronaldo.

4 One of his all-time heroes, and friend of the family, is former Wimbledon midfielder, and now Hollywood hardman, Vinnie Jones.

5 Former England manager Sven Goran Eriksson voted for Joe in the 2005-06 Footballer of the Year awards.

6 He supported Chelsea as a boy so was delighted to join The Blues for £6.6m in 2003.

7 In April 2006, *The Independent* voted Joe the fourth most happy person in the UK. A reported weekly salary of £60,000 must have something to do with it!

8 Joe made his England debut against Mexico in a friendly on May 25, 2001 and got his first goal against Serbia & Montenegro on June 3, 2003. At the start of this season he had got seven goals in 40 appearances.

9 Although boss Jose Mourinho now thinks Joe is a wicked player, back in the 2004-05 season he had a dig at his defensive failings: "I think he has two faces – one beautiful one and one that I don't like. He must keep one of them and change the other one."

10 Joe loves cars, his pride and joy being a Ferrari F360. If you fancy a brand new one yourself, there won't be much change from £200,000! A month playing for Chelsea should just about cover it!

KNOW YOUR FOOTBALL?

Time to test your knowledge again with more teasers and another giant crossword

SPOT THE DIFFERENCE

Can you spot the five changes in these two pictures?

FACE TO FACE

Look at the faces of the six well-known England players below and see if you can name them...

1

2

3

4

5

6

FOOTIE CROSSWORD

DOWN

1 Leigh - - -, has played for both Sheffield United and Wednesday (6)

2 Country that David Beckham left behind for the USA (5)

3 The Magpies' England striker, Michael - - - (4)

5 Nickname of Pride Park outfit, Derby County (4)

6 Dean - - -, West Ham striker sidelined throughout last season's relegation battle (6)

7 Blackburn - - -, club that gave Benni McCarthy his Premiership chance (6)

8 The Hammers' former Tottenham forward, Bobby - - -, who scored 11 Premiership goals last season (6)

11 Stamford Bridge club - 2007 Carling Cup winners (7)

15 Ex-Arsenal and England defender, Tony - - -, assistant to Harry Redknapp at Portsmouth last term (5)

16 Kevin - - -, Irish forward at Reading (5)

18 Swedish forward, Henrik - - -, loaned briefly to Manchester United last season (7)

21 Robbie - - -, Ewood Park Welshman who broke his leg in January (6)

22 Consistent Liverpool and Ireland full-back, Steve - - - (6)

23 Homeland of Arsenal midfielder, Freddie Ljungberg (6)

24 Leyton - - -, League One club from east London (6)

28 Sunderland's Trinidad and Tobago World Cup striker, Dwight - - - (5)

29 - - - Bromwich Albion, losing Championship play-off finalists 2006-07 (5)

30 Egyptian striker kept out of the Spurs side by Keane and Berbatov (4)

ACROSS

1 Lincolnshire club relegated to the Conference at the end of last season (6)

4 Didier - - -, Chelsea striker who topped the Premiership goal charts in 2006-07 (6)

9 Veteran Nigerian striker, Dele - - -, of Coventry City (7)

10 Man City defender, - - - Richards, given his first full England cap last term (5)

12 Darren - - -, England striker unable to stop Charlton's slide into The Championship (4)

13 Ex-Hammer, Jermain - - -, of Tottenham and England (5)

14 Barcelona's Portugal midfielder on target against Chelsea last term (4)

17 Nickname of Sheffield's red and white club (6)

19 Xabi - - -, Spaniard who helped Liverpool to the Champions League Final (6)

20 Former Reading defender, Linvoy - - - a rock in Pompey's defence (6)

22 London club who replaced boss, Chris Coleman, with Lawrie Sanchez (6)

25 Dennis - - -, manager who failed to keep Leeds in **The Championship (4)**

26 Man United defender Johnny - - - loaned to Sunderland last term (5)

27 Newcastle's England midfielder, Kieron - - -, (4)

31 Irish defender, Richard - - -, appointed Manchester City skipper last year (5)

32 If Wayne Rooney kicked a ball through your window you would need to call in a - - - (7)

33 Birmingham City's ex-Bolton defender, Bruno - - - (6)

34 Nottingham club led through the play-offs last season by Colin Calderwood (6)

1,000 NOT OUT!

Season 2006-07 marked a major landmark for football on TV. We look back at the vital facts involving live games on Sky...

Sky Sports showed their first live Premiership game on August 16, 1992. It was Nottingham Forest's 1-0 victory over Liverpool thanks to a strike from Teddy Sheringham (yes, he was around even then!).

Just three months earlier the satellite broadcaster had paid a staggering £304m to take live football off ITV in one of the most memorable TV rights battles ever seen.

Many pundits doubted that Sky could justify paying that amount of money. But just less than 15 years later, on May 10, 2007, they hit the landmark 1,000th live game when Tottenham and Blackburn Rovers drew 1-1 at White Hart Lane.

Commentator Martin Tyler, pundit Andy Gray and studio presenter Richard Keys have become legends in football broadcasting, with the studio anchor man now approaching 2,000 games in all competitions!

Other TV companies now battle for the rights to arguably the biggest league in the world... but Sky has set a new benchmark for the fan. Here are some of the highlights of those amazing 1,000 games...

Steed rides a tackle in the landmark at the Lane

There was a Keane in game 1,000...

...and another Keane in live game No.1!

Players warm up for the 1,000th Sky live game

1000th LIVE GAME Congratulations from BARCLAYS SKY SPORTS

Andy Gray, Teddy Sheringham and Richard Keys prepare for White Hart Lane's big game

Sky keep on trucking...

...and this is the view from the TV gantry!

The camerman's ready...

Fulham hit Norwich for six

STAT ATTACK

The milestones reached during Sky Sports' first 1,000 live games

TOTAL NUMBER OF GOALS
2,592 – an average of 2.592 per game

TOP SCORERS
52 Thierry Henry
44 Andy Cole
39 Alan Shearer
36 Robbie Fowler
35 Paul Scholes
33 Ruud Van Nistelrooy
31 Ryan Giggs
29 Ole Gunnar Solskjaer
26 Teddy Sheringham and
Jimmy Floyd Hasselbaink
25 Dwight Yorke
24 Michael Owen and Les Ferdinand
22 Robbie Keane and Mark Viduka
21 Wayne Rooney
20 Eric Cantona, Ian Wright
and David Beckham
19 Dennis Bergkamp

OWN GOALS
79

MOST OWN GOALS
3 Michael Duberry
2 Jamie Carragher (both v
Man United in 1999-00)

PENALTIES
107 (five each for Eric
Cantona and Frank Lampard)

HAT-TRICKS
23 (Dwight Yorke is the only
player to have scored two, for
Villa and Man United).

GOALLESS DRAWS
78

BIGGEST WIN
6-0 by Manchester United, Chelsea
and Fulham over Bolton, Barnsley
and Norwich respectively.

MOST GOALS IN ONE GAME
9 in the matches between Blackburn
Rovers and Sheffield Wednesday in
1997-98 (7-2 Blackburn) and the
4-5 at White Hart Lane won by
Arsenal in 2004-05.

Dwight Yorke – hat-trick king

Nine-goal thriller for Rovers and Wednesday

THE BEST GAME.... EVER!

MANY FANS AGREE and all three of Sky Sports' main men certainly do... this seven-goal thriller at Anfield was simply the best live game ever!

Supporters were left gripping the edge of their seats and gasping for breath as Kevin Keegan took his high flying Magpies to his former team in a top of the table clash.

The game got off to a flyer when Robbie Fowler scored in the first minute but by the interval the visitors had stunned The Kop by taking a 2-1 lead thanks to Les Ferdinand and David Ginola.

Anfield was rocking as Fowler got The Reds back to 2-2, but just minutes later Colombian Tino Asprilla restored the Geordies lead before Stan Collymore brought it level again with just over 20 minutes remaining.

A draw looked on the cards but, in time added on, Collymore slotted

Collymore strikes!

home the winner. Keegan's head slumped into his hands. His side's title hopes were dead and buried... and Special K's after-match interview included the famous rant at Fergie.

We loved it, just loved it! Who said TV football was boring?

Andy Gray summed up the night perfectly when he said: "I have just watched the match of the decade."

Thierry Henry – king of the live TV goals

FANTASY

England's finest

HEAD JOHN TERRY

The England and Chelsea captain is always prepared to put his head in where it hurts, as we saw last season when he clashed with Arsenal's Abou Diaby in the Carling Cup Final and had to be taken to hospital. JT is dominant in the air in either penalty area and provides a goal- scoring threat from set-pieces.

HEART JAMIE CARRAGHER

Most Liverpool fans would agree Carra is the heartbeat of their club. The committed centre-back always comes off the pitch with no regrets, knowing he has given his all. Carragher... probably the best Scouser in the world.

LUNGS STEVEN GERRARD

Stevie G's stamina level is awesome and he performs at great pace for well over 50 games every season, including internationals.

RIGHT LEG WAYNE ROONEY

His power and ability to smash the ball into the net from any distance or angle, with speed and accuracy, make him one of the deadliest finishers around.

FEET JOE COLE

Probably the most gifted English player of this generation. Joe's amazing range of tricks and skills and his superb natural ability means he is a vital ingredient.

BRAIN PAUL SCHOLES

The ginger gem is Manchester United's driving force in midfield. He starts passing moves from deep, plays deadly through balls and can leather it in from distance. The sharpness of his brain and ability to process information quickly and make the correct decisions nearly every time, make him the ideal choice.

MOUTH GARY NEVILLE

Gary Neville is loved by Manchester United fans and loathed by opposition supporters due to his committed nature, passion for United and the way he's constantly talking and organising his defence. Appointed United captain after Roy Keane's departure in 2005.

UPPER BODY EMILE HESKEY

The Wigan striker is built like a brick thingy and has great pace for a big man. With a chest the width of a barrel and shoulders as big as many WWE Superstars, the former England frontman is almost impossible to muscle off the ball. A real nightmare for defenders.

LEFT LEG MATTY TAYLOR

Power and accuracy are qualities the Portsmouth left-back has in abundance, and like Rooney, spectacular goals are par for the course.

PACE SHAUN WRIGHT-PHILLIPS

Chelsea's diminutive dynamo has natural speed and ability to carry the ball at pace. We'll also take the balance and low-centre of gravity that allow him to beat the opposition with ease.

FOOTBALLER

GM Goalie

The perfect outfield star is sorted, but we need a genetically modified keeper too. Here's our cloned custodian...

HEAD PAUL ROBINSON
The Spurs stopper has had to deal with his fair share of criticism over the past year but has coped well. The former Leeds United man's great mental strength would be a vital asset.

MOUTH JENS LEHMANN
Sometimes his mouth gets him into trouble with referees and winds up opposing players and fans, but it is a vital commodity for any top-class keeper. The Arsenal and Germany No.1 organises his defence and bellows out advice and instructions to others.

ARMS & HANDS PETR CECH
Probably the best keeper in the world at the moment. The Chelsea giant has the ability to save long and short range shots and keep hold of the ball.

HEIGHT AND STRENGTH DAVID JAMES
The experienced Pompey stopper was one of the best signings of last season. His displays showed exactly why he's earned 34 caps for England using his physical strength and experience to dominate his area.

LEGS BRAD FRIEDEL
Blackburn's all-American hero is one of the best in the business at coming off his line and denying an on-coming striker a shot at goal.

FINGERS JUSSI JAASKELAINEN
The Bolton man often makes spectacular finger-tip saves. The flexible Finn's agility and razor-sharp reactions make him one of the best in England.

PENALTY SAVES PEPE REINA
The Liverpool No.1 is the penalty saving specialist. His reputation has many players beaten before they even take their run up!

FEET EDWIN VAN DER SAR
Man United's NO.1 has great distribution with both his arms and feet, is cool and confident when the ball's on the deck and always deals with back-passes well.

AGILITY SHAY GIVEN
Newcastle's consistent performer since he joined in 1997. The Irish No.1 has amazing reactions and ability to claw the ball from his line when he appears to have been beaten.

57

FANTASY FOOTBALLER

Continental Clone

Now we check out the Premiership's foreign imports to give us a fantasy player with a Continental flavour...

HEAD NEMANJA VIDIC

The Serbian hard-man has added much needed grit to Man United's defence and it's no coincidence that his first full season at Old Trafford ended with The Red Devils picking up the Premier League trophy. Lethal in the air and has the bravery and guts to put his head and body on the line when needed.

HEART MICHAEL ESSIEN

The Ghana midfielder is the driving force of the current Chelsea side and often comments how he still has energy left over after games and that he could easily play another 90 minutes! Virtually unstoppable.

LUNGS DIRK KUYT

Liverpool's Dutch striker works his socks off, often dropping deep or going out on the flanks. Doesn't give defenders any rest.

RIGHT LEG MIKEL ARTETA

Everton's cultured midfielder is one of the Premiership's most improved players, and the accuracy of his right foot is one of the main reasons. The Spaniard has awesome ability from set-plays.

FEET CRISTIANO RONALDO

If you could add the technical ability and flight of foot that Cristiano possesses to our fantasy player he would be unplayable. At times last season Ronaldo was exactly that...

BRAIN DIMITAR BERBATOV

The talented Spurs forward is one of the cleverest players around and can read the runs of his team-mates, capitalise on defenders weaknesses and always seems a step ahead of the opposition.

MOUTH GEORGE BOATENG

The Boro skipper is an excellent organiser and leads the younger players around him by example with words of encouragement.

UPPER BODY DIDIER DROGBA

The Drog is a beast of a centre-forward who can brush mean defenders aside with ease thanks to his upper-body strength. Also has the pace and skill to hold up the ball and spin them at will.

LEFT LEG JOHN ARNE RIISE

The Liverpool powerhouse has one of the most explosive left-boots in world football, probably only second to the Brazil defender Roberto Carlos. Has enough power to frighten even the hardest of keepers.

PACE OBAFEMI MARTINS

Newcastle's Nigeria striker can tear top defences to shreds when he's in the mood and his excellent balance and low-centre of gravity make him extremely hard to tackle.

LET US TAKE YOU AROUND THE CLUBS

59

All you need to know about...
THE GUNNERS

STADIUM: The Emirates
CAPACITY: 60,000
MANAGER: Arsene Wenger
HIGHEST-EVER PREMIERSHIP FINISH: Champions 1998, 2002 and 2004
LOWEST-EVER PREMIERSHIP FINISH: 12th, 1995
LAST MAJOR TROPHY: FA Cup, 2005

SEASON 2006-07
PREMIERSHIP FINISH: 4th
TOP SCORER: Robin Van Persie 13

HIGH POINT: Beating Liverpool 6-3 at Anfield in the Carling Cup.
LOW POINT: Bowing out of the Champions League at the group stage having lost at home to PSV Eindhoven.

CURRENT STAR
Cesc Fabregas
The young Spaniard is maturing into one of the best all round midfielders in the European game. The 20-year-old has an excellent range of passing and orchestrates many of The Gunners flowing moves. He is vital to Arsenal's continued transformation into title challengers.

UNSUNG HERO
Gilberto Silva
The Brazil international quietly goes about his business with minimal fuss but maximum effort. Arsenal are a different team with Gilberto in the side as he allows the attacking players in front of him to get forward and express themselves. Gilberto also weighs in with some vital goals, and has an excellent record from the penalty spot.

HOT PROSPECT
Denilson
Another Samba star, is the latest whiz kid to roll off Monsieur Wenger's cosmopolitan production line. The skilful midfielder made his mark on the first-team last season and alongside Fabregas could form the basis of Arsenal's midfield for the next decade.

TRIVIA
The Gunners went on an amazing 49 game unbeaten run in the Premiership. It started on May 7, 2002 when they beat Southampton 6-1 and ended with a 2-0 defeat to Man United at Old Trafford on October 24, 2004!

CLASSIC YEARS
1994 With George Graham at the helm The Gunners won the European Cup Winner's Cup, beating Italian side Parma 1-0 in Copenhagen. Alan Smith scored the winning goal with a spectacular and rare left-footed volley.

1998 Arsenal claimed their first-ever Premiership title after defeating Everton at Highbury. Captain Tony Adams famously scored with a crisp left-foot volley. The club completed their second Double a few weeks later after defeating Newcastle United in the FA Cup Final.

2004 Arsene Wenger celebrated his third Premier League title as Arsenal boss when his side finished the season unbeaten playing some spectacular football along the way. The Gunner's were labelled The Invincibles and claimed their 13th league title.

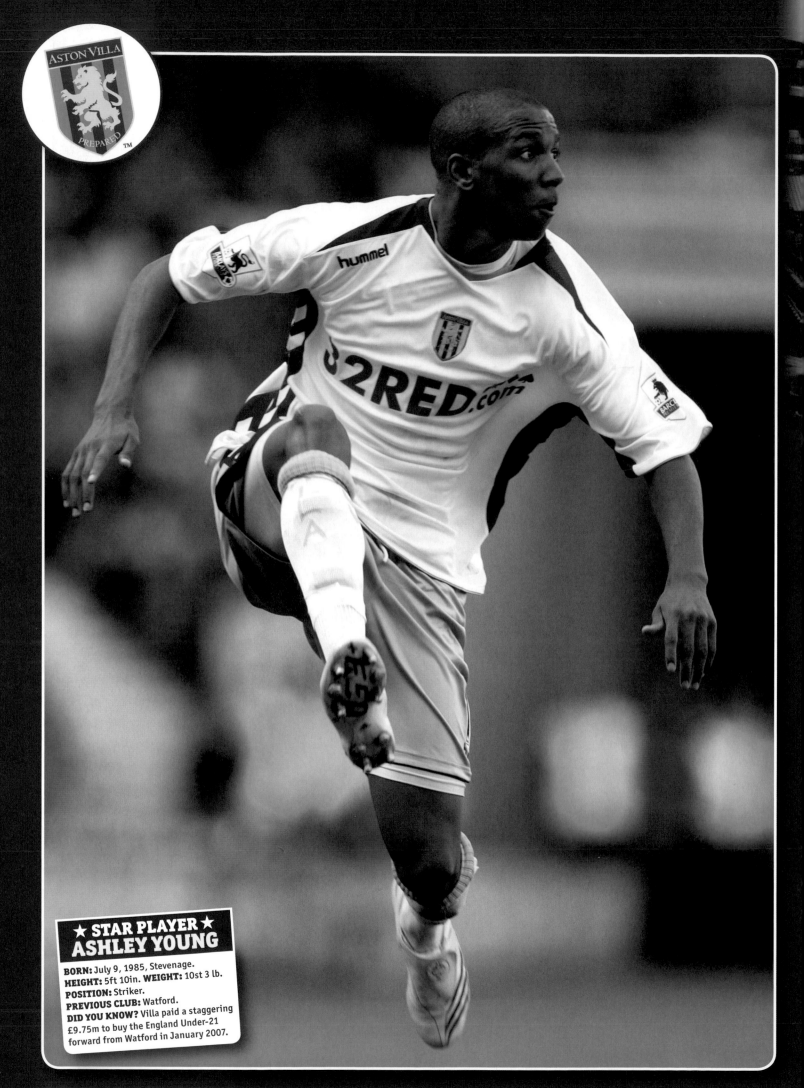

★ STAR PLAYER ★
ASHLEY YOUNG

BORN: July 9, 1985, Stevenage.
HEIGHT: 5ft 10in. **WEIGHT:** 10st 3 lb.
POSITION: Striker.
PREVIOUS CLUB: Watford.
DID YOU KNOW? Villa paid a staggering
£9.75m to buy the England Under-21
forward from Watford in January 2007.

All you need to know about...
THE VILLANS

STADIUM: Villa Park
CAPACITY: 42,573
MANAGER: Martin O'Neill
HIGHEST-EVER PREMIERSHIP FINISH: Runners-up, 1993
LOWEST-EVER PREMIERSHIP FINISH: 18th, 1995.
LAST MAJOR TROPHY: League Cup, 1996

SEASON 2006-07
PREMIERSHIP FINISH: 11th
TOP SCORER: Gabby Agbonlahor 10

HIGH POINT: The 1-1 draw with Chelsea when Gabby Agbonlahor's equalising goal grabbed an extremely credible point for The Villans at Stamford Bridge.

LOW POINT: Losing 3-1 at home against Manchester City in the league was a disappointing result for Martin O'Neill's side.

CURRENT STAR
Gareth Barry
Barry is Villa's Mr. Reliable and one of the top-flight's most consistent performers. Whether he's playing in defence, out wide, on the left or in central midfield, the England international is always one of The Villans' star performers. Barry scored eight league goals last term.

UNSUNG HERO
Olof Mellberg
The Sweden centre-half has been the most consistent of all Villa's foreign signings in recent years. His experience and ability to organise the defence were vital last season as younger defenders such as Liam Ridgewell and Gary Cahill made breakthroughs.

HOT PROSPECT
Craig Gardner
Gardner made an impact on the Villa first team on a regular basis at the end of last season. His range of passing and roving forward runs gave Martin O'Neill's midfield more drive and energy and the young Englishman also weighed in with two goals.

TRIVIA
In 1961 Villa won the first-ever League Cup Final, beating Rotherham 3-2 on aggregate.

CLASSIC YEARS
1981 Villa were crowned English Champions, finishing four points ahead of nearest rivals Ipswich Town. The star men of the era were legendary captain Dennis Mortimer and young England midfielder Gordon Cowans.

1982 The most famous day in Villa's history was May 26, 1982, when the Midlands side won the European Cup, beating German giants Bayern Munich in the final. Striker Peter Withe, the club's record signing for £500,000 at the start of that season, scored the winning goal as The Villans triumphed 1-0 on the night.

1993 Villa's debut season in the Premiership was their most successful to date, as they finished runners-up to Manchester United. Their entertaining and effective team included classy centre-back Paul McGrath, the battling qualities of Kevin Richardson in midfield and the lethal strike force of Welshman Dean Saunders and Dalian Atkinson.

All you need to know about...
THE BLUES

STADIUM: St. Andrews
CAPACITY: 30,016
MANAGER: Steve Bruce
HIGHEST-EVER PREMIERSHIP FINISH: 10th, 2004
LOWEST-EVER PREMIERSHIP FINISH: 18th, 2006
LAST MAJOR TROPHY: League Cup, 1963

SEASON 2006-07
CHAMPIONSHIP FINISH: Runners-up, automatic promotion.
TOP SCORER: Gary McSheffrey 16

HIGH POINT: The hard-fought 3-2 win away at Wolves played a significant part in The Blues gaining automatic promotion. Goals from Andy Cole, Cameron Jerome and Nicklas Bendtner and a vital last-minute penalty save from Colin Doyle sealed the victory.

LOW POINT: The 1-0 home defeat against mid-table Burnley in April came during a spell when The Blues' promotion hopes were flagging.

CURRENT STAR
Gary McSheffrey
A left-footed forward who can either play as a striker or a winger, McSheffrey has gone from strength-to-strength since his £4m move from Coventry City in 2006. If he can adapt to the pace of the Premiership an England cap wouldn't be out of the question.

UNSUNG HERO
Damien Johnson
Rated by Steve Bruce as his best-ever buy, the North

Ireland midfielder missed a chunk of last season with a broken jaw. Angered fans by throwing his captain's armband into the crowd when he was substituted early in the season. Won the supporters back with a vital equaliser against local rivals West Brom.

HOT PROSPECT
Colin Doyle
The Irish keeper was in fine form towards the end of last season for The Blues and kept the experienced and reliable Maik Taylor out of the side. Tall, with good feet and the ability to command his area, Doyle should rise to the challenge of the Premiership

this season and eventually take the place of Shay Given as the Republic's No.1.

TRIVIA
The most-capped player in Blue's history is Australian winger Stan Lazaridis. Stan earned 33 caps whilst on the books at St. Andrews.

CLASSIC YEARS
1963 The Blues won the League Cup, beating bitter local rivals Aston Villa 3-1 over two legs.

2002 Birmingham gained promotion to the Premiership after Steve Bruce's first season in charge. The side from the second city beat Norwich City on penalties in the play-off final at the Millennium Stadium with teenage Blues fan Darren Carter scoring the decider.

2004 Bruce guided Birmingham to their highest Premiership finish as his side claimed tenth. It was only the club's second full season in the Premier League and raised the supporters' expectations hugely.

★ STAR PLAYER ★
GARY McSHEFFREY

BORN: August 13, 1982, Coventry.
HEIGHT: 5ft 8in. **WEIGHT:** 10st 6 lb.
POSITION: Midfield-striker.
PREVIOUS CLUBS: Coventry City,
Stockport County (loan), Luton (loan).
DID YOU KNOW? Gary was the youngest
Premiership player after making his Coventry
debut at the age of 16 years and 198 days.

65

★ STAR PLAYER ★
DAVID DUNN

BORN: December 27, 1979,
Great Harwood, Lancashire.
HEIGHT: 5ft 9in. **WEIGHT:** 12st 3lb.
POSITION: Midfield.
PREVIOUS CLUBS: Blackburn Rovers
and Birmingham City.
DID YOU KNOW? David returned to Blackburn
in 2006 after three seasons at Birmingham.

All you need to know about... THE ROVERS

STADIUM: Ewood Park
CAPACITY: 31,367
MANAGER: Mark Hughes
HIGHEST-EVER PREMIERSHIP FINISH: Champions, 1995
LOWEST-EVER PREMIERSHIP FINISH: 19th, 1999
LAST MAJOR TROPHY: League Cup, 2002

SEASON 2006-07
PREMIERSHIP FINISH: 10th
TOP SCORER: Benni McCarthy 24

HIGH POINT: Taking Arsenal to a replay in the FA Cup and beating them 1-0 at Ewood Park after a 0-0 draw at The Emirates.

LOW POINT: Losing to Chelsea in the FA Cup semi-final at Old Trafford after forcing them into extra-time and creating enough chances to win the game.

CURRENT STAR
David Bentley
The young attacking-midfielder really came to the fore last season playing on the right of midfield for Mark Hughes' men. Bentley cruised through the challenges of most left-backs, creating countless chances for his colleagues and scoring a few belters of his own. Has been a regular at England Under-21 level and after a B team cap in May he will be keen to establish himself as a regular in the senior side.

UNSUNG HERO
Stephen Warnock
Warnock was signed from Liverpool during last season's January transfer window and his arrival seemed to add balance to Rovers' defence. He also provided a good attacking threat in tandem with left-winger Morten Gamst Pedersen. Stephen's solid displays played a major part in Blackburn's fine finish to the season.

HOT PROSPECT
Matt Derbyshire
The boyhood Rovers fan fulfilled his dreams as he made the breakthrough at Ewood Park last season. His bravery, ability to be in the right place at the right time and coolness in front of goal helped him notch nine goals in all competitions. Derbyshire has already been capped for England's Under 21 side and early comparisons to the great Gary Lineker may, like his finishing, not be too wide of the mark!

TRIVIA
Blackburn's record transfer fee received is the £17m Chelsea paid them for Irish winger Damien Duff in 2003.

CLASSIC YEARS
1992 Under the guidance of Kenny Dalglish, the Lancashire club achieved promotion to the Promised Land of the Premier League, beating Leicester City in the play-off finals at Wembley.

1995 With Dalglish still at the helm and owner Jack Walker backing him in the transfer market, Blackburn claimed the Premier League title in 1995, finishing above Manchester United after a dramatic last day of the season. The team's spine consisted of Tim Flowers in goal, Scotland defender Colin Hendry, midfielder David Batty and goals, goals, goals from the partnership labelled the SAS – Alan Shearer and Chris Sutton.

2002 Blackburn won the 2002 League Cup under Graeme Souness thanks to goals against Spurs from Matt Jansen and Andy Cole.

BOLTON

All you need to know about... THE TROTTERS

STADIUM: The Reebok
CAPACITY: 28,723
MANAGER: Sammy Lee
HIGHEST-EVER PREMIERSHIP FINISH: 6th, 2005
LOWEST-EVER PREMIERSHIP FINISH: 20th, 1996
LAST MAJOR TROPHY: FA Cup, 1958

SEASON 2006-07
PREMIERSHIP FINISH: 7th
TOP SCORER: Nicolas Anelka 12

HIGH POINT: Beating Arsenal 3-1 at home in November when former Gunner Nicolas Anelka grabbed two goals, including a cracking long-range effort.

LOW POINT: The 5-1 defeat against Middlesbrough at The Riverside was a particularly poor performance from The Trotters.

CURRENT STAR
Kevin Nolan
Nolan is the driving force in Bolton's midfield and will be vital to Sammy Lee's bid to keep the club progressing after Sam Allardyce's exit. Liverpool born Kevin works his socks off for the Wanderers cause and chips in with vital goals usually after arriving late in the box.

UNSUNG HERO
Nicky Hunt
The lanky right-back doesn't

get much attention from the press or fans but he has been quietly impressive since his debut in 2003. Hunt is one of the clubs more consistent and committed performers. He is strong in the air and more than capable on the ground.

HOT PROSPECT
Zoltan Harsanyi
The 20-year-old Slovakian striker was originally brought in on loan last season by then-boss Sam Allardyce and labelled as one for the future. After impressing new manager Sammy Lee, Harsanyi was given a three-year deal in May.

TRIVIA
British boxer and Olympic Silver medalist Amir Khan is a massive Bolton fan.

CLASSIC YEARS:
1958 Bolton won the FA Cup after beating Manchester United in the final thanks to two goals from the great Nat Lofthouse. The manager at the time was Bill Ridding.

2004 Bolton stunned football by finishing fourth in the Premiership and qualifying for the UEFA Cup. They also made it to the final of the League Cup, where they lost 2-1 to Middlesbrough.

2005 After several seasons spent establishing Bolton as a Premier League club, boss Sam Allardyce led The Trotters to a sixth place finish, their highest in Premiership history, and sealed qualification for Europe.

68

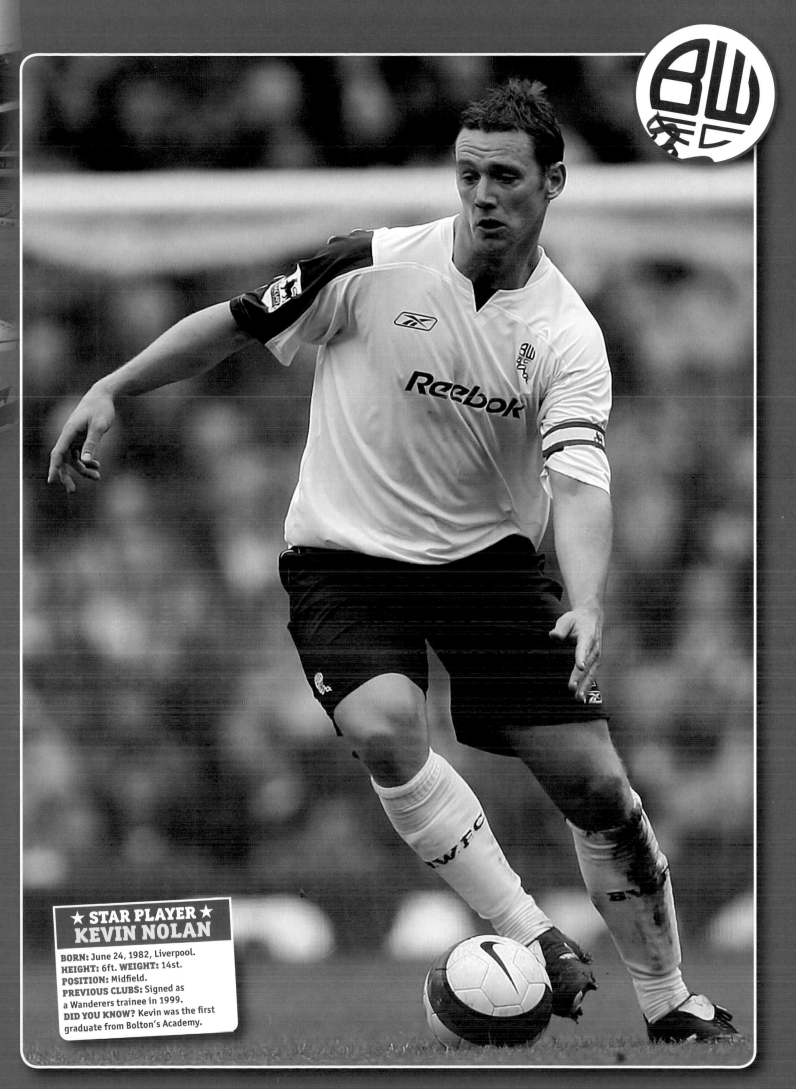

★ STAR PLAYER ★
KEVIN NOLAN

BORN: June 24, 1982, Liverpool.
HEIGHT: 6ft. **WEIGHT:** 14st.
POSITION: Midfield.
PREVIOUS CLUBS: Signed as a Wanderers trainee in 1999.
DID YOU KNOW? Kevin was the first graduate from Bolton's Academy.

★ STAR PLAYER ★
JOHN TERRY

BORN: December 12, 1980, Barking, Essex.
HEIGHT: 6ft 1in. **WEIGHT:** 14st 2lb.
POSITION: Central-defender.
PREVIOUS CLUBS: Chelsea since trainee.
DID YOU KNOW? Before making his breakthrough, captain JT was loaned out to Nottingham Forest for experience.

All you need to know about...
THE BLUES

STADIUM: Stamford Bridge
CAPACITY: 42,522
MANAGER: Jose Mourinho
HIGHEST-EVER PREMIERSHIP FINISH:
Champions, 2005 and 2006
LOWEST-EVER PREMIERSHIP FINISH:
14th, 1994
LAST MAJOR TROPHY:
Last season's FA Cup.

SEASON 2006-07
PREMIERSHIP FINISH:
Runners-up
TOP SCORER:
Didier Drogba 33

HIGH POINT: Winning the FA Cup against title rivals Manchester United at Wembley was some consolation for Mourinho and his charges for missing out in the league. They beat The Red Devils 1-0 thanks to Didier Drogba's extra-time winner.

LOW POINT: Losing out to Liverpool at the semi-final stage of the Champions League for the second time in three seasons will have hurt The Blues, especially as they were only defeated on penalties.

CURRENT STAR:
Didier Drogba
The Ivory Coast striker was Chelsea's main man last season and shouldered the team's goalscoring responsibility due to the poor form of Andriy Shevchenko and the inconsistency of young Salomon Kalou. The Drog was the Premiership's leading scorer and his unique brand of pace and aggression complemented by skill and amazing technical ability make him one of the most feared strikers in Europe.

UNSUNG HERO
Ricardo Carvalho

The Portugal defender was the only fit recognised centre-back at Jose Mourinho's disposal for much of last season, but his consistent performances and ability to break up attacks and move the ball on quickly were vital in sustaining Chelsea's title hopes.

HOT PROSPECT
Scott Sinclair
The exciting young winger made a name for himself on loan at Plymouth Argyle last term, where he scored a couple of memorable individual goals. Sinclair returned to the Bridge for the season's finale and made his league debut against Arsenal. Not that they need to worry about money, but this young man could certainly save Chelsea millions in the transfer market if he matches his great potential.

TRIVIA
Chelsea have qualified for European football for the last ten seasons.

CLASSIC YEARS
1955 The Blues were crowned Champions of the Football League for the first time in their history with the legendary Ted Drake as their manager.

1998 With Gianluca Vialli in charge, Chelsea claimed the League Cup, beating Middlesbrough 2-0 in the final. They also won the European Cup Winners Cup after a 1-0 victory over German side VFB Stuttgart, with the great Gianfranco Zola scoring the winning goal.

2005 Jose Mourinho guided Chelsea to their first title win for 50 years after his first season in charge at Stamford Bridge. The Blues finished with 95 points and were 12 points ahead of nearest rivals Arsenal. The stars were skipper John Terry, plus midfielders Claude Makelele and Frank Lampard.

All you need to know about...
THE RAMS

STADIUM: Pride Park
CAPACITY: 33,597
MANAGER: Billy Davies
**HIGHEST-EVER
PREMIERSHIP FINISH:**
8th, 1999
**LOWEST-EVER
PREMIERSHIP FINISH:**
19th, 2002
LAST MAJOR TROPHY:
Division One Champions, 1975

SEASON 2006-07
CHAMPIONSHIP FINISH:
Against the odds, finished
third in The Championship,
and then beat Southampton
over two legs to reach the
play-off final at Wembley.

TOP SCORER:
Steve Howard 19
HIGH POINT: The highlight
of the season was winning the
play-off final against West
Brom in May. Scotsman
Stephen Pearson scored the
goal in a 1-0 victory to seal the
contest dubbed as "the world's
richest game" due to the huge

amount of TV money available
to the winner.
LOW POINT: Missing out on
automatic promotion after
suffering a 2-0 defeat at
Crystal Palace at the tail
end of the season.

CURRENT STAR
Steve Howard
A physically imposing centre
forward both strong in the air
and excellent at holding up the
ball. Geordie Howard steam-
rollered through Championship
defences last season. Whilst he
may struggle to have a similar
impact on the Premiership,
plenty of top-flight defenders
will not look forward to battling
with the former Luton star.

UNSUNG HERO
DAVID JONES
The promising young
midfielder was snapped up by

Billy Davies from Manchester
United last season for £1m.
His assured performances in
the middle of the park and
ability to bomb forward and
deliver deadly free-kicks
make him one of County's
more dangerous performers.

HOT PROSPECT
Giles Barnes
The flying winger has plenty
in his locker, including pace,
trickery, vision and a deadly
finish. Bigger clubs have cast
a jealous eye at Derby's prized
asset and if he steps up to the
plate in the Premiership a big
money move and a chance with
England could be on the cards.

TRIVIA
Derby's youngest-ever player

is Lee Holmes who played
against Grimsby Town on
December 26, 2002 aged just
15 years and 268 days.

CLASSIC YEARS
1972 The Rams won the First
Division title for the first time
in their history with outspoken
genius Brian Clough at the
helm. Derby finished two
points ahead of challengers
Liverpool and Ipswich.

1975 Three years later Derby
were at it again, reclaiming
the Division One title, this time
with former player, and Brian
Clough signing, Dave Mackay
in charge of the team.

1999 Under the guidance of
Jim Smith The Rams achieved
their highest-ever Premiership
finish, 8th. With their new
Pride Park stadium built and
their top-flight status
apparently consolidated the
future looked bright for Derby.

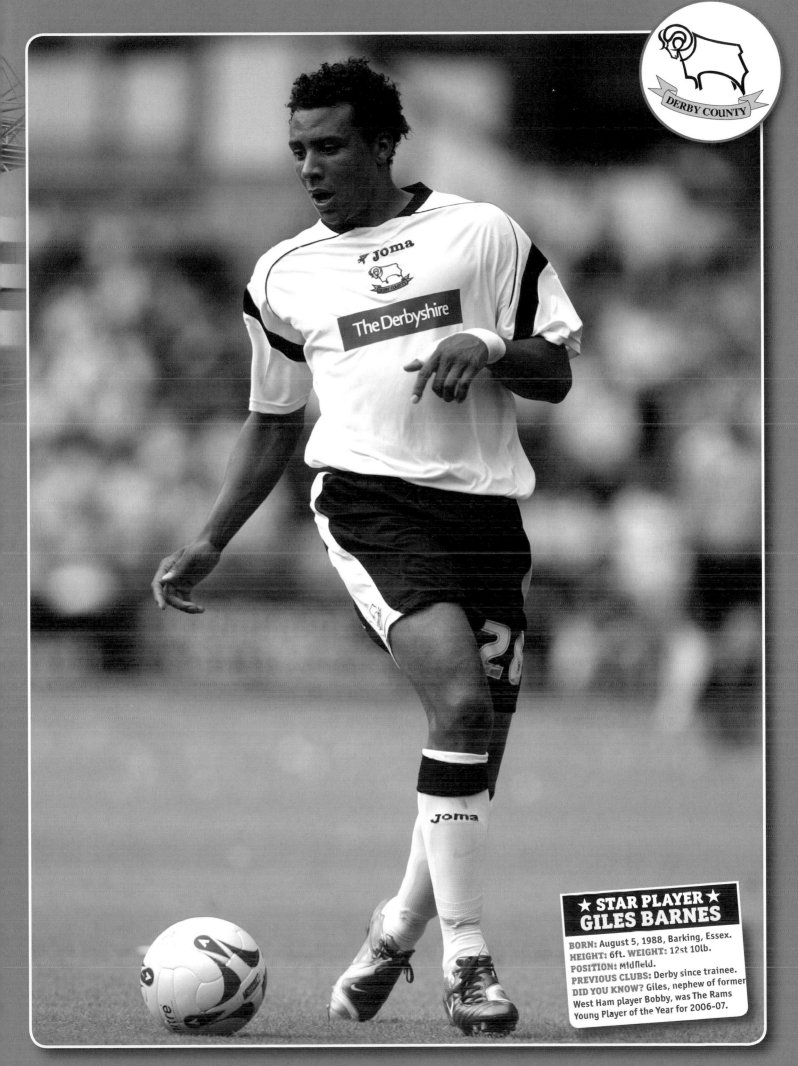

DERBY COUNTY

★ STAR PLAYER ★
GILES BARNES

BORN: August 5, 1988, Barking, Essex.
HEIGHT: 6ft. WEIGHT: 12st 10lb.
POSITION: Midfield.
PREVIOUS CLUBS: Derby since trainee.
DID YOU KNOW? Giles, nephew of former
West Ham player Bobby, was The Rams
Young Player of the Year for 2006-07.

73

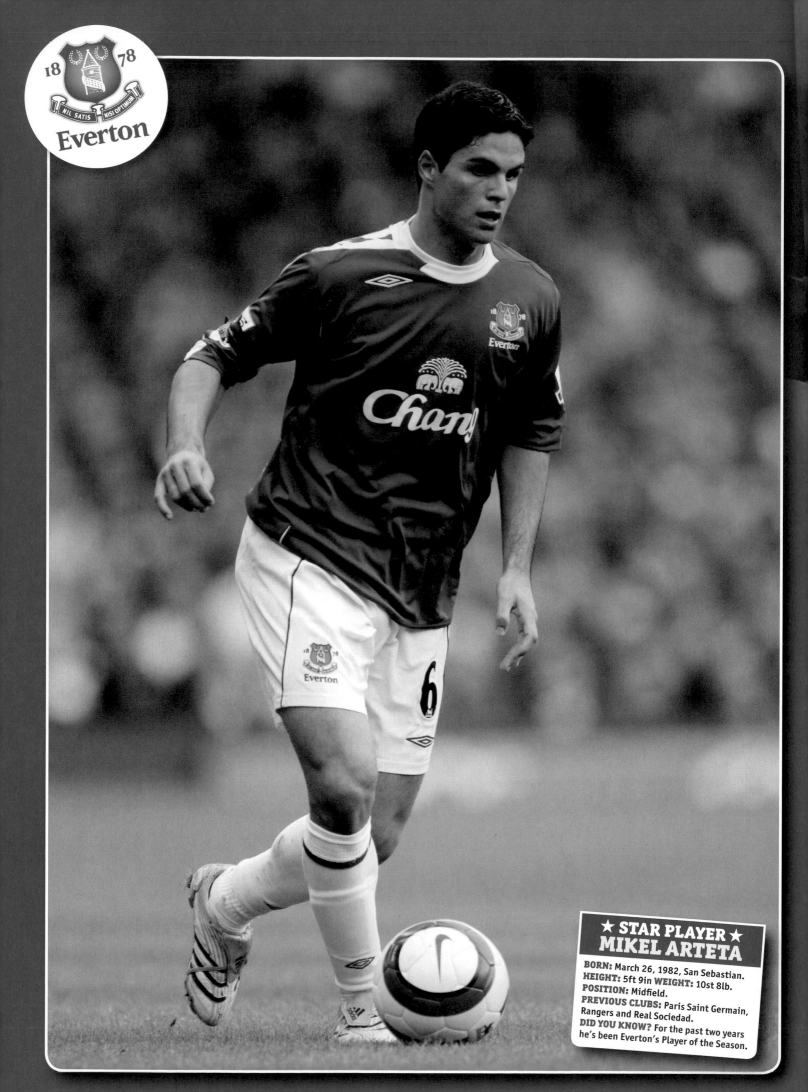

Everton

★ STAR PLAYER ★
MIKEL ARTETA

BORN: March 26, 1982, San Sebastian.
HEIGHT: 5ft 9in WEIGHT: 10st 8lb.
POSITION: Midfield.
PREVIOUS CLUBS: Paris Saint Germain, Rangers and Real Sociedad.
DID YOU KNOW? For the past two years he's been Everton's Player of the Season.

All you need to know about...
THE TOFFEES

STADIUM: Goodison Park
CAPACITY: 40,565
MANAGER: David Moyes
HIGHEST-EVER PREMIERSHIP FINISH:
4th, 2005
LOWEST-EVER PREMIERSHIP FINISH:
17th, 1994, 1998 and 2004
LAST MAJOR TROPHY:
FA Cup, 1995

SEASON 2006-07
PREMIERSHIP FINISH: 6th
TOP SCORER:
Andy Johnson 12

HIGH POINT: Beating Liverpool 3-0 at Goodison Park last September after destroying The Reds during a frantic first-half. Striker Andy Johnson did most of the damage as he bagged a brace with Aussie midfielder Tim Cahill also adding his name to the scoresheet.
LOW POINT: Bowing out of the FA Cup at home to Blackburn in an embarrassing 4-1 defeat.

CURRENT STAR:
Mikel Arteta
The supremely skilled Spain star took his game to another level last season as his craft and accurate passing created many of The Toffee's better moments during their impressive league campaign. Signed from Real Sociedad for £2m in 2005, the former Rangers man is one of the most naturally talented midfielders in the Premiership.

UNSUNG HERO
Leon Osman
Local lad Leon has been one of David Moyes most reliable performers in recent seasons. The attacking midfielder grabs

vital goals – often away from home – and his versatility gives his manager plenty of options in where to play him.

HOT PROSPECT
James Vaughan
The young striker started to realise some of his great potential last season and scored four goals after a sustained run in the side. Vaughan was part of the England Under-21 squad for the European Championships and has a bright future. James holds the record for the Premiership's youngest scorer having netted against Crystal Palace in 2005 aged just 16 years and 270 days.

TRIVIA
The Toffees have been Football League champions nine times.

CLASSIC YEARS
1985 With former player Howard Kendall in charge, Everton won the First Division title, finishing a staggering 13 points ahead of nearest challengers and local rivals Liverpool. In the same season they also won the European Cup Winners Cup, beating Austrian side Rapid Vienna 3-1 in the final.

1995 Joe Royle's team beat Manchester United 1-0 at Wembley to claim the FA Cup, for the club's only trophy of the modern era. Veteran striker Paul Rideout scored the scrappy winner to send the Goodison faithful into raptures.

2004 With canny Scot David Moyes at the helm, Everton claimed their highest ever Premiership finish beating Merseyside rivals Liverpool to fourth place and qualifying for the Champions League.

All you need to know about...
THE COTTAGERS

STADIUM: Craven Cottage
CAPACITY: 22,230
MANAGER: Lawrie Sanchez
HIGHEST-EVER PREMIERSHIP FINISH: 9th, 2004
LOWEST-EVER PREMIERSHIP FINISH: 16th, 2007
LAST MAJOR TROPHY: Division One champions, 2001

SEASON 2006-07
PREMIERSHIP FINISH: 16th
TOP SCORER: Brian McBride 12

HIGH POINT: Clint Dempsey's cool finish which sealed a 1-0 victory over Liverpool at Craven Cottage and ensured the club's Premiership status for another year.
LOW POINT: Losing 3-1 at home against fellow strugglers Man City left the faithful wondering if they'd survive.

CURRENT STAR
Brian McBride
The reliable American's goals have been vital to Fulham in recent seasons. Often playing as a lone striker, 35-year-old McBride's ability in the air and superb link-up play helped him earn last season's Player of the Year award and won him a further year's contract.

UNSUNG HERO
Moritz Volz
The versatile German can play in either defence or midfield and has been one of the London club's more consistent performers since his move from Arsenal in 2004.

HOT PROSPECT
Liam Rosenior
The 22-year-old defender or midfielder has now established himself in the Fulham first-team, but has the potential to develop his game further. His pace, strength and calmness on the ball mean he's ideally suited to the right-back role he made his own last season. Could soon emerge as a potential replacement for Gary Neville in the full England team.

TRIVIA:
Moritz Volz scored the 15,000th goal in Premier League history when he notched against Chelsea on December 30, 2006.

CLASSIC YEARS
1975 Under manager Alex Stock, The Cottagers reached the FA Cup Final for the first time in their history, only to lose out 2-0 to fellow Londoners West Ham.

2001 Frenchman Jean Tigana led Fulham to the Premiership after finishing top of the old First Division. The Cottagers amassed an amazing 101 points with current Man United striker Louis Saha in particularly impressive form.

2004 With former player Chris Coleman in charge the Craven Cottage outfit achieved their highest-ever Premiership finish as they claimed ninth place in the table.

★ STAR PLAYER ★
BRIAN McBRIDE

BORN: June 19, 1972, Chicago, USA.
HEIGHT: 6ft. **WEIGHT:** 12st 8lb.
POSITION: Striker.
PREVIOUS CLUBS: Wolfsburg, Columbus Crew, Preston North End, Everton.
DID YOU KNOW? Brian has appeared in the last three World Cups for the USA.

★ STAR PLAYER ★
STEVEN GERRARD

BORN: May 30, 1980, Whiston, Liverpool.
HEIGHT: 6ft. **WEIGHT:** 12st 5lb.
POSITION: Midfielder
PREVIOUS CLUBS: Liverpool since trainee.
DID YOU KNOW? Steven married long-time partner Alex Curran on June 16, 2007, flying in their wedding guests by helicopter!

All you need to know about...
THE REDS

STADIUM: Anfield
CAPACITY: 45,360
MANAGER: Rafa Benitez
HIGHEST-EVER PREMIERSHIP FINISH:
Runners-up, 2002
LOWEST-EVER PREMIERSHIP FINISH:
8th, 1994
LAST MAJOR TROPHY:
FA Cup, 2006

SEASON 2006-07
PREMIERSHIP FINISH: Third
TOP SCORER:
Peter Crouch 18

HIGH POINT: Beating big guns Barcelona over two-legs in the Champions League. The Reds humbled the Spanish giants 2-1 on their own patch and held on for a 1-1 draw at Anfield to send Ronaldinho and his mates crashing out of the tournament at the quarter-final stage.
LOW POINT: Getting played off the park at home to Arsenal in the League Cup as The Gunners trounced The Reds

6-3, with Julio Baptista, who often couldn't even finish a sandwich last season, managing to score four goals.

CURRENT STAR
Steven Gerrard
Stevie G is already a Liverpool legend thanks to his match-winning performances since the turn of the century. The dynamic midfielder has won the Champions League, UEFA Cup, FA Cup and League Cup with his local club and will now have an eye on the Premiership trophy. Gerrard is also one of England's star performers and will sweat blood for his teams.

UNSUNG HERO
Steve Finnan
The Republic of Ireland

defender is one of the most improved players in the Premiership. Since his move from Fulham in 2003, Steve has developed his defensive skills, added a more attacking threat to his game and become one of the most accurate crossers of the ball at Anfield. He has played at every level in England from the Conference to the Premier League.

HOT PROSPECT
Jack Hobbs
The former Lincoln City centre-back arrived at Anfield in 2005 after a successful trial. Can also play in midfield and was captain of Liverpool's victorious FA Youth Cup side last season.

TRIVIA
The Reds have won the Football League title a record 18 times and their five European Cup wins is a British record.

CLASSIC YEARS
1978 Liverpool became the first English club to reclaim the European Cup after defeating Belgian side Brugge 1-0 at Wembley. Scotland sensation Kenny Dalglish scored the winning goal with a neat chip from a tight angle.

1986 The Merseyside giants dominated throughout the 1980s and claimed the League and FA Cup Double in 1986 under player-manager Kenny Dalglish.

2005 Rafa Benitez's Reds claimed the fifth European Cup of the club's history after an amazing second-half fight-back when they levelled the score from 3-0 down against AC Milan, before eventually triumphing on penalties.

All you need to know about The...
THE CITIZENS

STADIUM: City of Manchester
CAPACITY: 47,500
MANAGER:
Sven Goran Eriksson
**HIGHEST-EVER
PREMIERSHIP FINISH:**
9th, 1993 and 2003
**LOWEST-EVER
PREMIERSHIP FINISH:**
18th, 1996 and 2001
LAST MAJOR TROPHY:
League Cup, 1976

SEASON 2006-07
PREMIERSHIP FINISH: 14th
TOP SCORER:
Joey Barton 7

HIGH POINT: The 1-0 home win over Arsenal early in the season. City showed real character and competitive spirit to beat The Gunners with Joey Barton scoring the winner from the penalty spot.

LOW POINT: Losing 4-0 away to lowly Wigan Athletic was a humiliating defeat for then-boss Stuart Pearce.

CURRENT STAR
Micah Richards
The young defender has made a real impact on the Premiership in recent seasons with his aggressive displays from right-back. Dangerous going forward, lightning quick and awesome in the air, Richards has the potential to be one of England's top players for the next decade and has already been capped four times by The Three Lions.

UNSUNG HERO
Richard Dunne
The Republic of Ireland defender has been a rock for City in recent seasons, and without the excellent partnership he formed with the now departed Sylvain Distin, the Eastlands club could well have tasted relegation. The former Everton man is strong in the tackle and dominant in the air.

HOT PROSPECT
Daniel Sturridge
Sturridge is a young man with a massive reputation after some impressive performances for City's youth teams. Daniel, the nephew of former professional strikers Dean and Simon could be the answer to City's goal-scoring problems if given a run in the side.

TRIVIA
The biggest-ever FA Cup attendance outside Wembley was recorded at Maine Road. In the sixth round, on March 3, 1934, some 84,569 fans watched Man City v Stoke City, the best crowd for any English club apart from a cup final.

CLASSIC YEARS
1968 Manchester City were crowned League champions for only the second time in their history under the stewardship of Joe Mercer. The Blues pipped local rivals Manchester United to the title by two points.

1969 City beat Leicester 1-0 at Wembley to claim the FA Cup with Neil Young scoring the winning goal and legendary captain Tony Book lifting the famous trophy.

1976 City's last major honour was the League Cup they claimed in 1976, after beating Newcastle United 2-1. Former player Tony Book was boss and Dennis Tueart, until recently a City director, hit the winner.

★ STAR PLAYER ★
RICHARD DUNNE

BORN: September 21, 1979, Dublin.
HEIGHT: 6ft 2in. **WEIGHT:** 15st 10lb.
POSITION: Central-defender.
PREVIOUS CLUB: Everton.
DID YOU KNOW? Richard, who almost left City two years ago, has been Player of the Season for the last three years.

★ STAR PLAYER ★
WAYNE ROONEY

BORN: October 24, 1985, Liverpool.
HEIGHT: 5ft 10in. **WEIGHT:** 12st 13lb.
POSITION: Striker.
PREVIOUS CLUB: Everton.
DID YOU KNOW? Wayne used to be a
keen boxer and one of his big mates is
welterweight champion Ricky Hatton.

All you need to know about...
RED DEVILS

STADIUM: Old Trafford
CAPACITY: 76,000
MANAGER:
Sir Alex Ferguson
**HIGHEST-EVER
PREMIERSHIP FINISH:**
Champions 1993, 1994,
1996, 1997, 1999, 2000,
2001, 2003 and 2007
**LOWEST-EVER
PREMIERSHIP FINISH:**
Third 2004, 2005 and 2006
LAST MAJOR TROPHY:
Last season's Premiership title

SEASON 2006-07
PREMIERSHIP FINISH:
Champions

TOP SCORERS:
**Cristiano Ronaldo and
Wayne Rooney both 23**
HIGH POINT: Coming back
from two goals down away to
Everton to claim a 4-2 win on
the same day that Chelsea
stuttered against Bolton.
United fans will look back on
that weekend as the one which
sealed their ninth Premiership

title. The 7-1 win against
Italian giants Roma in the
Champions League quarter-
final also stands out.
LOW POINT: The 2-1 defeat
against Arsenal at the Emirates
when Robin Van Persie grabbed
a late equaliser and Thierry
Henry nodded in the winner
during stoppage time after
United had led with just a
few minutes remaining. The
semi-final exit at the hands of
AC Milan was also hard to take.

CURRENT STAR
Cristiano Ronaldo
The Portugal ace was the
catalyst for United's success
last season, answering his
critics with his ability, assists
and finishing. Ronaldo notched
17 league goals from the wing
and his amazing skills kept
fans entertained from August

to May. Cristiano was awarded
for his displays with the PFA
Player and Young Player of the
Year awards as well as being
named the Football Writers'
Player of the Year.

UNSUNG HERO
John O'Shea
The Irishman's versatility was
extremely useful for Sir Alex
Ferguson last season. He fitted
in well along the back four and
excelled in midfield. O'Shea
also popped up with two vital
goals in United's title run-in as
he netted twice on Merseyside,
once at Everton and the winner
against Liverpool.

HOT PROSPECT
Guiseppe Rossi
The American-born striker has
represented Italy at Under-21
level and despite an excellent

reputation and a glowing
evaluation from Fergie
regarding his finishing, Rossi is
yet to make the breakthrough
at Old Trafford. Spent a
frustrating time on loan at
Newcastle, but enjoyed a more
productive spell with Parma
when his goals helped save the
Serie A side from relegation.

TRIVIA
When Paul Scholes scored for
England against Tunisia in the
World Cup in France in 1998,
he was the first United player
to score at the finals since
Jesper Olsen notched for
Denmark in 1986.

CLASSIC YEARS
1968 United became the first
English side to win the
European Cup on an emotional
night at Wembley. United
defeated Benfica 4-1 after
extra-time.

1994 The team claimed their
first-ever Double, retaining
the title and beating Chelsea
4-0 in the FA Cup Final.

1999 The year United won the
Treble of the
European
Cup, Premier
League and
FA Cup.

All you need to know about... THE BORO

STADIUM: The Riverside
CAPACITY: 35,120
MANAGER: Gareth Southgate
HIGHEST-EVER PREMIERSHIP FINISH: 7th, 2005
LOWEST-EVER PREMIERSHIP FINISH: 21st, 1993
LAST MAJOR TROPHY: League Cup, 2004

SEASON 2006-07
PREMIERSHIP FINISH: 12th
TOP SCORER: Mark Viduka 19

HIGH POINT: Beating Chelsea 2-1 at The Riverside thanks to a last-minute winner from Aussie hit-man Mark Viduka.
LOW POINT: Losing 2-0 at home to Manchester City in the league.

CURRENT STAR
Aiyegbeni Yakubu
The Nigeria powerhouse has been in top form for Boro since his £7.5m transfer from Portsmouth in 2005. The Yak's pace and presence up front make him one of more feared forwards in the top-flight, and following Mark Viduka's departure he will be expected to score even more goals for Gareth Southgate's men.

UNSUNG HERO
George Boateng
Club captain and midfield anchor-man, Holland international Boateng has been a consistent performer for Boro since his £5m move from Aston Villa in 2002. George breaks up attacks, organises and encourages the younger players around him and will be a vital voice on the pitch now former skipper Gareth Southgate bosses the team from the sidelines.

HOT PROSPECT
Lee Cattermole
Midfield battler who can also play a bit with a varied range of passing. Cattermole is one of the many products from Boro's youth academy to

graduate to the first-team. The local lad is tipped as a future England star.

TRIVIA
Boro's record transfer fee paid is £8.1m to Italian's Empoli for striker Massimo Maccarone in 2002. It wasn't a good deal!

CLASSIC YEARS
1995 Boro gained promotion to the Premiership in player-manager Bryan Robson's first season in charge, having won the First Division title. Norway striker Jan Aage Fjortoft's goals were crucial that campaign.

2004 With current England boss Steve McClaren in charge, Middlesbrough won the first major trophy in their history as they defeated Bolton 2-1 in the League Cup Final. Dutch winger Bolo Zenden netted the winner from the spot.

2005 With McClaren still at the helm the Teessiders enjoyed their best Premiership campaign as they claimed seventh spot in the final league table, qualifying for the UEFA Cup in the process.

★ STAR PLAYER ★
JONATHAN WOODGATE

BORN: January 22, 1980, Middlesbrough.
HEIGHT: 6ft 2in. **WEIGHT:** 12st 6lb.
POSITION: Central-defender.
PREVIOUS CLUBS: Leeds, Newcastle, Real Madrid.
DID YOU KNOW? Boro paid Real Madrid £7m to bring Woody back to his home-town, boyhood heroes after a successful loan during season 2006-07.

★ STAR PLAYER ★
MICHAEL OWEN

BORN: December 14, 1979, Chester.
HEIGHT: 5ft 8in. **WEIGHT:** 11st 12lb.
POSITION: Striker.
PREVIOUS CLUBS: Liverpool,
Real Madrid.
DID YOU KNOW? Michael is the fourth-
highest goal-scorer ever for England.

All you need to know about...
THE MAGPIES

STADIUM: St. James' Park
CAPACITY: 52,387
MANAGER: Sam Allardyce
HIGHEST-EVER PREMIERSHIP FINISH: Runners up, 1996 and 1997
LOWEST-EVER PREMIERSHIP FINISH: 13th, 1998 and 2007
LAST MAJOR TROPHY: Inter City Fairs Cup, 1969

SEASON 2006-07
PREMIERSHIP FINISH: 13th
TOP SCORER: Obafemi Martins 17

HIGH POINT: The Magpies' victory away to Spurs was one of their better results of the season and showed the genuine potential of the players on the books at St. James' Park.
LOW POINT: The 1-0 defeat at home to Manchester City in March didn't go down too well with the Newcastle fans, and signalled the beginning of the end for previous boss Glenn Roeder.

CURRENT STAR
Michael Owen
The England striker has endured an injury plagued start to his career on Tyneside so far and the Gallowgate faithful are yet to see the best of the former Liverpool man. If he stays fit, Owen's goals could take Newcastle up to the higher reaches of the Premiership where they belong.

UNSUNG HERO
Shola Ameobi
Shola is another striker who has had more than his fair share of injury problems in recent years. Often playing when less than 100 per cent fit, Ameobi was out for the

majority of last season, and the period of rest and recovery should serve him well for the future. His strength and ability in the air should certainly suit new boss Sam Allardyce's style.

HOT PROSPECT
Andy Carroll
Young Geordie striker saw some action last season and will be hoping to make more of an impact this time round. Carroll is an old fashioned target man and has just agreed a new contract on Tyneside.

TRIVIA
Keeper Shay Given is The Magpies' most-capped player and the joint record cap holder for the Republic of Ireland with 80 international games.

CLASSIC YEARS
1955 Newcastle won the FA Cup Final after beating Manchester City 3-1, with the legendary Jackie Milburn grabbing one of the goals. The manager that year was Duggie Livingstone.

1969 The Magpies won the Inter City Fairs Cup, now known as the UEFA Cup, with a 6-2 victory over two legs against Hungarian side Ujpest Dozsa. The stars of the side were striker Wynn Davies, Bobby Moncur and Frank Clark.

1995 Kevin Keegan's side played some of the most entertaining football in Premiership history with the likes of David Ginola, Rob Lee and Les Ferdinand all in the side. Despite a 12-point advantage at one stage in the season, The Magpies faltered and finished as league runners-up to Manchester United.

All you need to know about...
POMPEY

STADIUM: Fratton Park
CAPACITY: 20,220
MANAGER: Harry Redknapp
HIGHEST-EVER PREMIERSHIP FINISH:
9th, 2007
LOWEST-EVER PREMIERSHIP FINISH:
17th, 2006
LAST MAJOR TROPHY:
Division One title, 2003

SEASON 2006-07
PREMIERSHIP FINISH: 9th
TOP SCORER:
Nwankwo Kanu 12

HIGH POINT: Beating Manchester United 2-1 at Fratton Park thanks to a neat Matt Taylor finish and comical own-goal from Rio Ferdinand.
LOW POINT: Losing 4-2 at bottom-placed Watford just days after beating Manchester United was hard for manager Harry Redknapp to take.

CURRENT STAR
Matt Taylor
The dynamite-filled left boot of Matt Taylor scored some memorable long-range goals last season, and his all round game made him one of the Premiership's most consistent performers. Another good season should see him given a chance with England.

UNSUNG HERO
Gary O'Neil
The club captain goes about

his business quietly and effectively and can always be relied upon to give at least a seven out of ten performance. O'Neil has a great engine, is strong in the tackle and gets forward to good effect.

HOT PROSPECT
Daryl Fordyce
A Northern Ireland youth international striker who spent time on loan at Bournemouth last season. Fordyce once scored four goals in a game for his country's Under-19 side, against Serbia in 2005.

TRIVIA
Pompey's highest league scorer in one season is Guy Whittingham who notched 42 times in Division One during the 1992-93 season.

CLASSIC YEARS:
1939 Pompey claimed the FA Cup for the first and only time in their history defeating Wolves 4-1 at Wembley.

1950 The South Coast club reclaimed the First Division title they had won the season before under the guidance of manager Jimmy Rae.

2003 With Harry Redknapp as the gaffer, Portsmouth reached the Premiership for the first time in their history. They had won the Division One title with veteran former England midfielder Paul Merson instrumental in their success.

★ STAR PLAYER ★
DAVID JAMES

BORN: August 1, 1970, Welwyn.
HEIGHT: 6ft 5in. **WEIGHT:** 15st 7lb.
POSITION: Goalkeeper.
PREVIOUS CLUBS: Watford, Liverpool,
Aston Villa, West Ham, Man City.
DID YOU KNOW? David is a good painter
who has sold some of his pictures.

★ STAR PLAYER ★
KEVIN DOYLE

BORN: September 18, 1983, Adamstown.
HEIGHT: 5ft 11in. **WEIGHT:** 12st 6lb.
POSITION: Striker.
PREVIOUS CLUB: Cork City.
DID YOU KNOW? Steve Coppell drank a few Guinnesses when he bought Kevin and didn't recall much about the deal!

All you need to know about...
THE ROYALS

STADIUM: The Madejski
CAPACITY: 24,200
MANAGER: Steve Coppell
HIGHEST-EVER PREMIERSHIP FINISH: 8th, 2007
LOWEST-EVER PREMIERSHIP FINISH: 8th, 2007
LAST MAJOR TROPHY: Championship title, 2006

SEASON 2006-07
PREMIERSHIP FINISH: 8th
TOP SCORER: Leroy Lita 14

HIGH POINT: The 6-0 thrashing of West Ham at the Madejski Stadium on New Year's Day. Kevin Doyle grabbed two.
LOW POINT: Losing 2-0 at home to Watford in their final home game was a disappointing end to an excellent season.

CURRENT STAR
Kevin Doyle
The young Republic of Ireland striker's rise to stardom to recent years has been remarkable. In 2005 he was playing for Cork City and now he's a feared Premier League forward and full international.

UNSUNG HERO
James Harper
The former Arsenal man partnered Steven Sidwell in the Reading midfield last season. His performances maybe weren't as noticeable as Sidwell – who left for Chelsea – but his contribution was just as important.

HOT PROSPECT
Shane Long
Another young Irishman who made the move from Cork City at the same time as Kevin Doyle. Long is three years younger than Doyle and his first-team chances have been limited in recent season, but his undoubted promise was confirmed last season as he notched four goals.

TRIVIA
The Royals' highest league goalscorer in a season was Ronnie Blackman who hit 39 in 1951-52 in the old Division Three South.

CLASSIC YEARS
1994 The Royals claimed the Division Two Championship and promotion to the First Division (now Championship) under the guidance of Scottish-born manager Mark McGhee.

2006 Reading reached the Premiership for the first time ever after finishing top of the pile in The Championship. Steve Coppell's men led from the front for most of the season with the foundations built on a strong defence allowing the striking talents of Dave Kitson, Leroy Lita and Kevin Doyle to shine.

2007 Reading's debut Premiership campaign was simply amazing. They attacked teams, playing in an organised yet adventurous manner. Steve Coppell led the Berkshire club to some impressive cup results and his side finished eighth, just missing out on a first appearance in Europe.

All you need to know about...
BLACK CATS

STADIUM:
The Stadium of Light
CAPACITY: 49,000
MANAGER: Roy Keane
HIGHEST-EVER PREMIERSHIP FINISH:
7th, 2000 and 2001
LOWEST-EVER PREMIERSHIP FINISH:
20th, 2003 and 2006
LAST MAJOR TROPHY:
FA Cup, 1973

SEASON 2006-07
CHAMPIONSHIP FINISH:
Champions
TOP SCORER:
David Connolly 13

HIGH POINT: The 5-0 thrashing of Luton Town at Kenilworth Road which sealed the Championship title for Roy Keane's men.
LOW POINT: Losing 3-1 at Southend in August kept The Black Cats rooted to the bottom of the table and in need of a miracle... step up Roy Keane.

CURRENT STAR
Dean Whitehead
The talented midfielder has been Sunderland's most reliable performer in recent years and was one of the only shining lights of their last spell in the Premiership two seasons ago. Committed, calm on the ball and full of running, Whitehead has improved further under the guidance of Roy Keane.

UNSUNG HERO
Liam Miller
Signed from Manchester

United last season, Miller impressed The Black Cats' faithful with some top quality performances and vital goals. The Irish international is another midfielder who can benefit from Keane's experience and motivation.

HOT PROSPECT
Anthony Stokes
The Republic of Ireland striker joined Sunderland in the January transfer window from Arsenal after an impressive loan spell in Scotland with Kilmarnock. Stokes showed glimpses of his ability last season and has the potential to be a regular scorer in the Premiership.

TRIVIA
The Black Cats record transfer fee paid is £8m to Rangers for Norway striker Tore Andre Flo in 2002.

CLASSIC YEARS
1973 Bob Stokoe's side claimed the FA Cup after beating Leeds United 1-0 in the final thanks to a goal from Ian Porterfield and the goalkeeping heroics of Jim Montgomery.

1999 With Peter Reid as gaffer the Wearsiders gained promotion to the Premiership after winning the First Division title with a record 105 points. Strikers Kevin Phillips and Niall Quinn were the stars of the show.

2001 Reid led Sunderland to their second successive seventh-place finish in the top-flight and once again had Kevin Phillips to thank for scoring most of the goals.

★ STAR PLAYER ★
DEAN WHITEHEAD

BORN: January 12, 1982, Abingdon.
HEIGHT: 5ft 11in. **WEIGHT:** 12st 6lb.
POSITION: Midfield.
PREVIOUS CLUB: Oxford United.
DID YOU KNOW? Dean joined Sunderland in June 2004 for an initial £150,000, which has since risen to £325,000 due to appearances.

TOTTENHAM HOTSPUR

MANSION

★ STAR PLAYER ★
ROBBIE KEANE

BORN: July 8, 1980, Dublin.
HEIGHT: 5ft 9in. **WEIGHT:** 12st 2lb.
POSITION: Striker.
PREVIOUS CLUBS: Wolves, Coventry, Inter Milan, Leeds United.
DID YOU KNOW? Robbie is the Republic of Ireland's record scorer with 29 goals.

All you need to know about...
SPURS

STADIUM: White Hart Lane
CAPACITY: 36,237
MANAGER: Martin Jol
HIGHEST-EVER PREMIERSHIP FINISH: 5th, 2006 and 2007
LOWEST-EVER PREMIERSHIP FINISH: 15th, 1994.
LAST MAJOR TROPHY: League Cup, 1999.

SEASON 2006-07
PREMIERSHIP FINISH: 5th
TOP SCORER: Dimitar Berbatov 23

HIGH POINT: Beating Chelsea 2-1 at White Hart Lane thanks to goals from Michael Dawson and Aaron Lennon. The win ended Chelsea's hoodoo over Spurs and Blues fans can no longer label the ground "Three Point Lane".
LOW POINT: Exiting the UEFA Cup at the quarter-final stage to Spanish side Sevilla with former Tottenham striker Fredi Kanoute bagging one of the crucial goals.

CURRENT STAR
Dimitar Berbatov
The Bulgaria striker was one of the players of last season and as he settled into the English game he transformed Spurs' early season wobbles into a solid campaign in the league and cup competitions. With an amazing coolness, world-class ability and a deadly finish, Berbatov could help Spurs break into the top four on a regular basis.

UNSUNG HERO
Michael Dawson
The tall centre-back had to shoulder much of Spurs'

defensive responsibilities last season as captain Ledley King missed most of the campaign with injury. His dominance in the air and in the tackle and improving ability on the ball make him vital to manager Martin Jol's future plans.

HOT PROSPECT
Tom Huddlestone
Signed from Derby in 2005, Huddlestone is gradually coming to the fore at Spurs. The physically imposing midfielder put in some extremely composed displays last season and scored several spectacular long range efforts.

TRIVIA
Tottenham's all-time top league goalscorer is Jimmy Greaves who hit the back of the net on 220 occasions for the North London club.

CLASSIC YEARS
1961 With the legendary Bill Nicholson in charge, Spurs became the third English club to claim the League and FA Cup double as they beat Leicester City 2-0 at Wembley.

1984 Spurs claimed the UEFA Cup for the second time in their history beating Belgian side Anderlecht 4-3 on penalties after 1-1 draws in both legs of the final.

1991 Tottenham won the FA Cup in a memorable final which saw midfielder Paul Gascoigne stretchered off injured, Gary Lineker miss a penalty and Nottingham Forest defender Des Walker score Tottenham's winner past his own keeper! Terry Venables was the man in charge and Gary Mabbutt the victorious skipper who lifted the trophy.

All you need to know about...
THE HAMMERS

STADIUM: Upton Park
CAPACITY: 34,500
MANAGER: Alan Curbishley
HIGHEST-EVER PREMIERSHIP FINISH:
5th, 1999
LOWEST-EVER PREMIERSHIP FINISH:
18th, 2003
LAST MAJOR TROPHY:
FA Cup, 1980

SEASON 2006-07
PREMIERSHIP FINISH: 16th
TOP SCORER:
Bobby Zamora 11

HIGH POINT: Winning 1-0 at Old Trafford on the last day of the season to guarantee their Premiership safety thanks to a classy finish from the talismanic and controversial Argentina striker Carlos Tevez.
LOW POINT: The 6-0 thrashing handed out by

Premiership new-boys Reading at the Madejski Stadium.

CURRENT STAR
Dean Ashton
The dangerous target-man missed all of last season with a nasty ankle injury picked up whilst training with England, and West Ham certainly struggled without him. When fit he is one of the most promising English forwards around with his ability in the air, strength on the ball and impressive touch.

UNSUNG HERO
Robert Green
The former Norwich City keeper performed miracles as The Hammers narrowly avoided relegation last season, with

his display in the 1-0 victory at Arsenal one of the finest goalkeeping performances in Premiership history. But his contribution was overshadowed by Tevez, who was just as vital to the club.

HOT PROSPECT
Mark Noble
Local lad Mark went on loan to Ipswich, but forced his way into Alan Curbishley's Hammers side on his return. As the season progressed he played a major part in the club's relegation battle, linking the midfield and attack and popping up with vital goals. A boyhood West Ham fan, he also appeared for England during last summer's UEFA Under-21 tournament.

TRIVIA
The Hammers have only employed ten other managers since Syd King was their first boss in 1902.

CLASSIC YEARS
1965 West Ham claimed their first major European Trophy defeating TSV Munich 1860 2-0 in the final of the Cup Winners Cup at Wembley with the late great Bobby Moore captaining their side.

1980 John Lyall's Hammers won the FA Cup after beating Arsenal 1-0 in the final thanks to Trevor Brooking's famous diving header.

1986 With John Lyall still at the helm, the Upton Park club were third in the First Division, their highest-ever finish in English football's top-flight. The Irons' dangermen were Tony Cottee and Frank McAvennie who formed a potent striking partnership.

★ STAR PLAYER ★
ROBERT GREEN

BORN: January 18, 1980, Chertsey, Surrey.
HEIGHT: 6ft 3in. **WEIGHT:** 14st 9lb.
POSITION: Goalkeeper.
PREVIOUS CLUB: Norwich City.
DID YOU KNOW? Rob fancies being a journalist when he hangs up his boots.

WEST HAM UNITED

WIGAN ATHLETIC

★ STAR PLAYER ★
CALEB FOLAN

BORN: October 26, 1982, Leeds.
HEIGHT: 6ft 2in. **WEIGHT:** 14st 7lb.
POSITION: Striker.
PREVIOUS CLUBS: Leeds, Rushden (loan), Hull (loan), Chesterfield.
DID YOU KNOW? League Cup goals for Chesterfield against Man City, West Ham and Reading earned Caleb his move.

All you need to know about...
THE LATICS

STADIUM: The JJB Stadium
CAPACITY: 25,000
MANAGER: Chris Hutchings
HIGHEST-EVER PREMIERSHIP FINISH:
10th, 2006
LOWEST-EVER PREMIERSHIP FINISH:
17th, 2007
LAST MAJOR TROPHY:
None

SEASON 2006-07
PREMIERSHIP FINISH: 17th
TOP SCORER:
Emile Heskey 8

HIGH POINT: The dramatic final day victory over Sheffield United at Bramall Lane which ensured the club's Premiership status. Former Blade David Unsworth scored from the spot to send United down and keep Wigan up.
LOW POINT: The 3-0 home defeat against West Ham was a tame performance from The Latics and one which looked to have sealed their relegation before a miracle turnaround in the closing weeks.

CURRENT STAR
Emile Heskey
The former England striker was one of the main reasons that Wigan stayed up last term. He finished as the club's top scorer with eight goals and led the line superbly. Emile also gave a heroic performance in the final day win over Sheffield United, dropping back into defence to clear every cross and corner with the bravery and intensity he needs to show more often.

UNSUNG HERO
Denny Landzaat
The midfielder was quietly effective last term after

signing from AZ Alkmaar following his appearances in the World Cup finals for Holland. He scored a couple of spectacular long-range goals.

HOT PROSPECT
Tomasz Cywka
The 19-year-old Poland midfielder joined Wigan in the summer of 2006 despite attracting interest from German giants Bayern Munich. Cywka enjoyed a successful spell on loan at Oldham Athletic last season and will now be hoping to get a chance in the Wigan first-team.

TRIVIA
New manager Chris Hutchings was promoted from assistant after Paul Jewell left at the end of last season. The same thing happened when Jewell left Bradford City in 2000.

CLASSIC YEARS
1999 With John Deehan as manager The Latics claimed the Auto Windscreens Shield at Wembley, beating Millwall 1-0 and Paul Rogers scoring the winning goal.

2005 Paul Jewell led Wigan to the Premiership as the side finished second in The Championship with the goals of Jason Roberts and Nathan Ellington playing a major part in their success.

2006 The Latics shocked English football by finishing tenth in the Premiership at the first time of asking and also reaching the final of the League Cup, where they lost 4-0 to Manchester United.

HEROES PAST AND PRESENT

We highlight the players who have recently impressed the fans at each of The Championship clubs and take a look at some of their heroes from the past...

BARNSLEY

PRESENT: BRIAN HOWARD

The left-sided midfielder was signed from Swindon in 2005. A threat with his crossing and passing, he also contributes goals. After playing an important part in the Oakwell club's promotion of 2006, the 24-year-old certainly didn't look out of place in The Championship.

PAST: NEIL REDFEARN

The much-travelled midfielder was instrumental in promotion to the Premiership in 1997. A favourite due to his lung-bursting runs and scoring ability.

BLACKPOOL

PRESENT: SCOTT VERNON

The impressive young striker was signed from Oldham in 2005 and played a major part in The Tangerines' improvement under Simon Grayson.

PAST: ALAN BALL

The great Alan Ball began his glittering career with Blackpool in 1962. After four seasons and winning the World Cup in 1966, the battling midfielder joined Everton. Sadly passed away last April.

BRISTOL CITY

PRESENT: SCOTT MURRAY

A skilful right-winger who in his second spell with The Robins after rejoining from Reading in 2004. First arrived at Ashton Gate in 1997 for £150,000 from Aston Villa and joined The Royals in 2003. Scored a long-range goal against Middlesbrough in the FA Cup last season.

PAST: BRIAN TINNION

Tinnion gave great service to the club over 12 years, both as a player and as a manager. Played left-back and left-wing and hit the winner at Anfield that knocked Liverpool out of the FA Cup in 1994.

BURNLEY

PRESENT: ANDY GRAY

The Scotland striker arrived last summer and has continued to add to his impressive goals tally. After mixed spells with Sheffield United and Sunderland the former Leeds trainee seems to be back to his best under Burnley boss Steve Cotterill. Has been capped twice.

PAST: ANDY PAYTON

A life-long Burnley fan, Payton joined The Clarets in 1998 from Huddersfield Town. The prolific striker established himself as a firm fan's favourite at Turf Moor and scored 81 goals in 178 appearances in all competitions.

CARDIFF CITY

PRESENT: STEPHEN McPHAIL

The midfielder arrived on a free from Barnsley in summer of 2006 and played 43 Championship games in his first season. The Republic of Ireland man raised his game with the move to Wales and showed the class which made him a Premiership player with Leeds just a few years ago, although his achievements were shaded by the scoring of Michael Chopra.

PAST: NATHAN BLAKE

Cardiff-born and a boyhood Bluebirds fan, Blake played at Ninian Park between 1990 and 1994 and scored 35 goals in 131 league appearances. The powerful striker, whose former clubs include Sheffield United, Bolton Wanderers and Blackburn Rovers, also earned 29 caps for Wales.

CHARLTON ATHLETIC

PRESENT: LUKE YOUNG

Young has been a consistent performer at right-back for The Addicks since his move from Tottenham for an initial fee of £3m in 2001. Solid at the back and with the pace and vision to pose a threat going forward, his performances have earned him international recognition for England.

PAST: ROB LEE

The former Newcastle and England midfielder made his name at Charlton in the 1980s and 1990s and represented the club for 11 seasons before catching the eye of Kevin Keegan in 1992. Lee played more than 200 games for Charlton and is still fondly remembered by The Valley faithful.

COLCHESTER UNITED

PRESENT: KEMAL IZZET

The brother of former Leicester and Birmingham star Muzzy, Kem is one of the U's longest-serving players. The popular midfielder has been at Layer Road since joining from Charlton Athletic in 2001. He was a vital part of the 2005-06 promotion-winning side and was a virtual ever-present last season as United held their own in The Championship.

PAST: MARK KINSELLA

Former Republic of Ireland midfielder and an experienced Premiership campaigner with Charlton and Aston Villa. Kinsella first made a name for himself at Layer Road in the early 1990s. Energetic and competitive with an eye for a pass, he is one of the club's all-time greats.

COVENTRY CITY

PRESENT: ELLIOT WARD

The promising young central-defender arrived at the Ricoh Arena in 2006 having graduated from the famous youth academy at West Ham United.

An uncompromising yet stylish defender, Ward was one of the few plus points in a disappointing campaign for Coventry last season.

PAST: MICKY GYNN

An energetic and whole-hearted midfielder who spent almost ten years playing for The Sky Blues and was part of the FA Cup-winning team of 1987. His work ethic and tenacity made him a favourite with the Coventry fans who were gutted when he was sold to Stoke.

CRYSTAL PALACE

PRESENT: LEON CORT

The physically intimidating centre-back is brother of former Wimbledon striker Carl. Leon made an impressive start to his Palace career when Peter Taylor took him to Selhurst Park following his own move from Hull City. Commanding in both penalty areas, Cort added pace and steel to the defence.

PAST: MARK BRIGHT

Partnered Ian Wright in one of the most lethal strike forces the club has ever seen. Bright was top scorer at Selhurst Park on three separate occasions during his six-year spell at Palace. Dominant in the air and more than capable on the ground, the Stoke-born striker left The Eagles in 1992 to become an Owl at Sheffield Wednesday. Now working as a pundit and commentator for BBC Radio.

HULL CITY

PRESENT: NICKY BARMBY

Former England striker and a star Premiership performer for Tottenham, Middlesbrough, Everton and Liverpool. Barmby has been turning in match-winning performances for his home-town team, Hull City, since 2004. He has helped The Tigers to successive promotions from League Two to One, and League One to The Championship.

PAST: DEAN WINDASS

Starred for Hull in the early 1990s and has now returned for his third spell following a loan from Bradford towards the end of last season. Made his name as an aggressive and direct striker in the lower leagues but also played for Aberdeen and Middlesbrough.

IPSWICH TOWN

PRESENT: ALAN LEE

Tall and physically imposing striker who joined Ipswich at the start of last season for a bargain £100,000 from Cardiff City. Lee repaid the faith manager Jim Magilton showed in him by bagging the goals that helped ensure Championship survival for The Tractor Boys. He has been capped eight times by the Republic of Ireland.

PAST: JIM MAGILTON

The club's current manager was a stalwart for Town throughout his eight-year spell at the club as a player. A combative yet skilful midfielder, Magilton played a major part in all of their successes in the 1990s. He also represented Northern Ireland on 52 occasions and starred in the Premiership for Southampton.

LEICESTER CITY

PRESENT: MATTY FRYATT

A goal-scoring sensation at Walsall, Fryatt signed for Leicester in 2006 and looks to have a bright future ahead of him. The young striker had his fair share of injury problems last season, but has shown glimpses of the top-class player he could become.

PAST: STEVE CLARIDGE

A real journeyman of a striker who clocked up his 1,000th League appearance whilst playing for Bournemouth last season. It was at Leicester that Claridge enjoyed the most successful period of his career, with his socks pulled down and his shirt hanging out, he scored play-off and League Cup Final winning goals for The Foxes. Claridge left the club for home-town side Portsmouth in 1998.

NORWICH CITY

PRESENT: DARREN HUCKERBY

Quick, skilful and a defender's nightmare, Huckerby has been Norwich's dangerman for the last five seasons. His goals helped fire The Canaries into the Premiership in 2004 and his ability to run with the ball at pace and pick out a pass have made him a great provider of goals too. Can play as a striker or on the wing.

PAST: JEREMY GOSS

Will be remembered for his spectacular long-range effort against Bayern Munich in the Olympic Stadium in a 2-1 Canaries' victory during their 1994 UEFA Cup campaign. Goss was a hard-working midfielder who enjoyed getting forward and became a real fan's favourite during his 12-year spell at Carrow Road. Also played international football for Wales.

PLYMOUTH ARGYLE

PRESENT: PAUL WOOTON

Wooton has been at Argyle for his entire career and has earned himself legendary status amongst the Home Park faithful. The club captain, who can operate in defence or midfield, has been inspirational for The Pilgrims since 1994. Led Plymouth's two title-winning sides of 2004 and 2005.

PAST: PAUL MARINER

One of the greatest players to have worn the green of Argyle, the multi-talented forward started his - old in 1973. Ipswich boss Bobby Robson bought him in 1976 and Mariner went on to play for Arsenal and England.

PRESTON NORTH END

PRESENT: DANNY PUGH

The former Man United midfielder went to Leeds in the deal that saw Alan Smith move to Old Trafford but less than two seasons later moved to North End for £250,000. He was boss Paul Simpson's first signing and has proved more than capable on the left or in central midfield. His manager has predicted that he has the ability to go a lot further if he keeps working hard at improving his game.

PAST: DAVID EYRES

The flying winger, voted into the Preston fans' team of all-time, only played at Deepdale for three seasons. Joined the club from Burnley for £80,000 in 1997, aged 34, and won a Division Two medal in 2000.

QPR

PRESENT: GARETH AINSWORTH

Tricky winger and a firm favourite at Loftus Road, Ainsworth joined QPR in 2003 following his release from Cardiff City. Made a name for himself whilst at Lincoln City and also played in the Premiership with Wimbledon.

PAST: ANDY SINTON

Another speedy winger whose direct style, dribbling skills and ability to cross the ball made him one of the stars of Ranger's Premiership era in the early 1990s. The Geordie went on to play for Sheffield Wednesday and was capped 12 times by England.

SCUNTHORPE UNITED

PRESENT: ANDY CROSBY

Defensive lynchpin and captain Andy has turned in influential performances for The Iron since 2004. Commanding in the air and tough in the tackle, he is an old school centre-back who will relish playing at a higher level after last season's promotion from League One.

PAST: ALEX CALVO-GARCIA

The battling Spanish midfielder stayed eight-years after arriving at Glanford Park in 1996. Best remembered for his winning goal in the 1999 Division Two play-off final against Leyton Orient at Wembley. Retired at the end of season 2003-04.

SHEFFIELD UNITED

PRESENT: ROB HULSE

The hard-working striker was signed from Leeds at the start of last season and scored eight Premiership goals, before a nasty injury ruled him out for the season and dashed The Blades' survival hopes. Rob will be aiming to get back to full fitness and fire the Yorkshire club back into the top-flight.

PAST: DANE WHITEHOUSE

Local lad dedicated to the cause during his time at Bramall Lane. Was a one-club man and who turned down chances to move. Provided excellent displays on the left side of the pitch either in defence or midfield, before injury cut his career short in 1997.

SHEFFIELD WEDNESDAY

PRESENT: CHRIS BRUNT

Vastly skilled Northern Ireland winger with a sweet left foot and the ability to score from long-range. Brunt has been at Hillsborough since 2004 and was part of the play-off winning side of 2005. Rumours persist that several Premiership sides have the former Middlesbrough man in their sights. Belfast-born he has made more than 100 league appearances for The Owls.

PAST: DAVID HIRST

A classic English-style centre-forward, Hirst scored the goals to propel Wednesday back to the highest level in the early 1990s and helped them to regular top-half Premiership finishes. Bagged 149 goals in 348 league games and scored one goal in the three games he played for England.

SOUTHAMPTON

PRESENT: GRZEGORZ RASIAK

The Poland striker had spells with Derby and Spurs before moving to St. Mary's in 2006. He's almost scored a goal every other game for Saints proving a £2m bargain buy. The Polish community in Southampton turn out in force to support their fellow countryman.

PAST: MATT LE TISSIER

Known as "Le God" by Saints fans, Matt Le Tissier was one of the most skilful players to have graced the Premiership and almost certainly the greatest player in Southampton's history. His eye for the spectacular and deadly finishing saved the club from relegation for more than a decade. One-club Le Tiss also earned eight caps for England.

STOKE CITY

PRESENT: STEVE SIMONSEN

Simonsen cemented his reputation as one of the best keepers outside of the Premiership with his performances last season. The former Everton stopper was one of the main reasons behind The Potters excellent defensive record in 2006-07.

PAST: GORDON BANKS

England's finest-ever keeper played for Stoke in the 1960s and 1970s. Banks was England's No.1 in 1966 when Sir Alf Ramsey's legendary side claimed the World Cup. He joined City following the World Cup after Leicester City made him available for transfer, due to a young Peter Shilton's emergence at the club. The goalkeeping legend left Stoke in 1972 after 194 league games.

WATFORD

PRESENT: MARLON KING

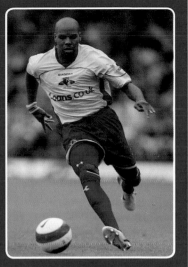

Marlon will be chomping at the bit to play regular football again after missing much of The Hornets' Premiership campaign due to injury. The talented striker will want to continue his partnership with Darius Henderson and fire Aidy Boothroyd's charges back to the big league.

PAST: JOHN BARNES

The Liverpool legend made his breakthrough at Watford during the 1980s as a skilful winger. The Jamaican-born star was one of the most talented players of his generation who scored 11 goals as he earned 79 England caps. Part of the Watford side that lost 2-0 in the 1984 FA Cup Final to Everton. John played 296 times for Watford and hit 85 goals.

WEST BROM

PRESENT: CURTIS DAVIES

A promising centre-back signed by former boss Bryan Robson in 2006, Davies has gone from strength to strength, and is destined to be a top performer at Premiership level for years to come. Bigger clubs like Spurs and Newcastle have been linked with the solid defender who had a transfer request refused.

PAST: BOB TAYLOR

A goal-scoring legend at The Hawthorns and fan's favourite throughout his time with the club. Taylor is to Baggies fans what Steve Bull is to Wolves supporters. Super Bob had two spells with West Brom, from 1992 to 1998 and 2000 to 2003 and played more than 300 games for Albion. The County Durham-born star also enjoyed a successful few seasons with Bolton Wanderers.

WOLVES

PRESENT: MICHAEL KIGHTLY

The rise of the right-winger has been meteoric since his release from Southend in 2005. Made a name for himself in non-League with Grays Athletic and soon attracted the attention of Wolves and Man United. But Fergie was beaten to Kightly's signature by Mick McCarthy in January. The young Englishman recently agreed a new deal at Molineux as the big clubs again began sniffing.

PAST: STEVE BULL

One man will forever by linked to Wolves – Steve Bull. Signed from bitter local rivals West Brom in 1986, he scored 306 goals in 504 games for the club. Bully never played in the top-flight yet still represented England, and was part of the Italia 90 squad.

A LEAGUE OF THEIR OWN

Here are the stars who've recently made a name for themselves with League One clubs...

BOURNEMOUTH WARREN CUMMINGS
The Scottish left-back joined from Chelsea in 2003 after impressing on loan. Despite some bad luck with injuries Cummings has been a consistent performer.

BRIGHTON DEAN HAMMOND

The energetic midfielder is now an integral part of the Brighton set up having progressed through the youth system. Hammond is dangerous going forward and one of the first names on the manager's team sheet.

BRISTOL ROVERS RICHARD WALKER
Former Aston Villa front-man who joined Bristol Rovers in 2004 from Blackpool. He scored 21 goals for the Pirates in 2005-06 and was again a constant threat to League Two defences last term.

CARLISLE PAUL THIRLWELL
After a successful loan, the former Sunderland trainee joined on a permanent basis last January from Derby. The holding midfielder broke up attacks and passed the ball well for The Cumbrians last term.

CHELTENHAM TOWN JOHN FINNIGAN
Club captain John Finnigan signed from Lincoln City in 2002 and is one of the most consistent performers at Whaddon Road. The midfielder was instrumental in the club's promotion to League One in 2006.

CREWE NICKY MAYNARD
A sharp striker who was another product of Crewe's legendary youth academy, Maynard scored 16 goals for Alex last season and will be vital next term now scoring sensation Luke Varney has left the club.

DONCASTER PAUL HEFFERNAN
Improving striker who knows how to find the back of the net. Heffernan has impressed for Rovers since his move from Bristol City in 2005. The Ireland Under-21 star reached double-figures in the league last season.

GILLINGHAM NICKY SOUTHALL
A legend at the Priestfield Stadium and one of the more talented performers in League One. Nicky is currently enjoying his third spell with the Kent club and offers a goal threat from midfield.

HARTLEPOOL RICHARD BARKER
The former Sheffield Wednesday striker joined Pools during last season's January transfer window and his goals helped ensure Hartlepool's immediate return to League One following relegation the previous campaign.

HUDDERSFIELD TOWN ANDY BOOTH

A tall, tough and talented striker and one of Huddersfield's greatest servants, who had his testimonial season last term. During his two spells with the club, he has scored vital goals and worked tirelessly.

LEEDS UNITED EDDIE LEWIS

The USA winger joined from Preston North End in 2005 and was one of the few bright sparks during last season's failed battle against relegation. Had a brief spell with Fulham five years ago.

LEYTON ORIENT MATT LOCKWOOD

The experienced left-back, who has played for Bristol Rovers and QPR, ended the last campaign as the club's Player of the Year for the second successive season. Lockwood is now in his tenth year at Brisbane Road.

LUTON TOWN LEON BARNETT

The promising defender made his senior Hatters' debut aged just 16 as he appeared as a substitute in the 2002 LDV Vans final at the Millennium Stadium. His best position is in the centre of defence but he is also capable of playing as a full-back.

MILLWALL NEIL HARRIS

A real fox in the box striker, Harris is in his second spell with the club having rejoined from Nottingham Forest. Neil survived his battle with testicular cancer in 2001 and is now showing signs of the devastating form evident in his first spell at the New Den.

NORTHAMPTON ANDY KIRK

A prolific scorer in Scotland with Hearts and in England with Boston United, Kirk joined Northampton in 2005 for £150,000. The Irishman hasn't scored as many as he'd have liked for The Cobblers but he always works hard for the team and shows his genuine class.

NOTTINGHAM FOREST KRIS COMMONS

Having supported the club as a boy, Commons arrived at the City Ground in 2004 from Stoke. Has a deadly left foot and the ability to play at a higher level.

OLDHAM RICHARD WELLENS

Former Manchester United trainee Wellens joined Oldham on a free transfer from Blackpool in 2005. He won the fans' Player of the Season award in 2005-06 and continued to impress Athletic supporters at Boundary Park last term.

PORT VALE GEORGE PILKINGTON

The former Everton defender has been a rock for Vale since he joined in 2003 after he was surprisingly released by Everton. His committed displays have been rewarded with the captain's armband. The 6ft tall star can play anywhere across the back and scores a few goals.

SOUTHEND KEVIN MAHER

The Shrimpers' midfielder was Player of the Year at the end of last year, a fitting reward for almost ten years' of dedication to the Essex side. Kevin has now played more than 400 games for United since a free transfer from Tottenham in 1998.

SWANSEA CITY LEE TRUNDLE

Lee joined The Swans in 2003 from Welsh rivals Wrexham. He isn't the fastest striker around, but he sure knows how to score!

SWINDON CHRISTIAN ROBERTS

The Welshman, a former Bristol City striker, swapped one set of Robins for another when he joined Swindon Town in 2004 for £50,000.

TRANMERE CHRIS GREENACRE

The experienced striker arrived in 2005 after a frustrating spell at Stoke. Greenacre has always scored in the lower leagues and notched 18 for Tranmere in his first full season at the club. Continued his fine form last term.

WALSALL MARTIN BUTLER

An experienced striker who arrived on a free transfer from Rotherham in 2006 for his second spell with the club. Played an important part in The Saddler's successful promotion campaign last season.

YEOVIL TOWN CHRIS COHEN

A product of West Ham's famous academy, Cohen joined in 2006 after a successful loan. The energetic midfielder is as comfortable defending as he is going forward and is a firm fans' favourite.

BARGAIN BASEMENT

Having seen what The Championship and League One sides have to offer, take a look at the League Two heroes of the present and very recent past...

ACCRINGTON STANLEY ROBBIE WILLIAMS

Stanley's longest-serving player has entertained fans before the Millennium having joined the club in 1999. The defender learned his trade at Liverpool and has eight various winner's medals with Accrington.

BARNET LIAM HATCH

The tall striker was signed from non-league side Gravesend and Northfleet for £24,000 in 2003. Despite suffering a serious cruciate ligament injury on his debut his work-rate has made him a favourite.

BRADFORD CITY DAVID WETHERALL

The veteran defender has seen it all! He joined the club in the Premiership in 1999 and has suffered three relegations. One of The Bantams' better performers in that period and even caretaker manager last season.

BRENTFORD PAUL BROOKER

The talented midfielder joined The Bees from Reading in 2005 having also played for Fulham, Brighton and Leicester. A reliable performer at Griffin Park, who can play on either wing, and often scores some spectacular goals.

BURY DAVE CHALLINOR

Former Tranmere defender famed for his amazing long throws. Joined Bury in 2004 and his strength and experience have held the club's back-line together.

CHESTER CITY PHIL BOLLAND

The tall centre-back spent three months on loan at Chester during 2001-02 before the move was made permanent. Returned from Peterborough last term.

CHESTERFIELD MARK ALLOT

The reigning Player of the Year continued to impress last season, despite the club's disappointing league campaign. Joined from Oldham in 2002 and has been one of the club's most consistent performers.

DAGENHAM AND REDBRIDGE PAUL BENSON

The young striker was spotted by Daggers boss John Still whilst playing for Essex side White Ensign, whom he scored 96 goals for in two years. Joined in 2005 and his goals shot the club to the Conference title.

DARLINGTON JULIAN JOACHIM

Starred in the Premiership for Leicester City and Aston Villa but joined The Quakers from Boston United in 2006. But the class is still very evident and Joachim is one of the most dangerous strikers at this level.

GRIMSBY TOWN NICK FENTON

Former Manchester City youngster who joined Grimsby from Doncaster Rovers in 2003. The 27 year-old can play at right-back or in the centre of defence.

HEREFORD UNITED STEVE GUINAN
An experienced and mobile striker now in his second spell with the Bulls, Guinan recently rejoined permanently after impressing on loan last season.

LINCOLN CITY JAMIE FORRESTER
Vastly experienced forward who has had more clubs than hot dinners and has found the back of the net on a regular basis for most of them!

MACCLESFIELD TOWN DAVID MORLEY
Centre-half Morley is club captain and was influential as the club avoided relegation last season. The ex-Man City trainee is strong and dominant in the air.

MANSFIELD TOWN MATT HAMSHAW
The former Sheffield Wednesday man has made a big impression since he joined in 2006 from Stockport. Added pace and guile to the midfield.

MK DONS DEAN LEWINGTON
The former Wimbledon defender was Player of the Year in 2006 and was also a key performer last term when he played more than 50 games. Offers the club determination and is also a big danger at set pieces.

MORECAMBE MICHAEL TWISS
The experienced striker joined Morecambe from Chester during 2003-04 and has played an integral part in the club's promotion to the Football League.

NOTTS COUNTY JASON LEE

Became a legend in the early 1990s thanks to a dodgy haircut labelled "Pineapple Head". Has since proved a more than capable striker with physical presence.

PETERBOROUGH GUY BRANSTON
The Leicester City youth product joined Posh in 2006 from Oldham. A powerful centre back, he became a fan's favourite thanks to his committed displays.

ROCHDALE CHRIS DAGNALL

Dagnall arrived at Spotland in 2006 after a £15,000 transfer from Tranmere Rovers. The Liverpool-born, nippy striker reached double-figures for The Dale last campaign.

ROTHERHAM UNITED PAUL HURST
One of the Millers' longest-serving players and a true one club man, Hurst has been turning in consistent performances at left-back since he made his debut for Rotherham in 1993. Just 5ft 5in tall, the Sheffield-born defender has played more than 400 games.

SHREWSBURY TOWN DEREK ASAMOAH
Lightning quick striker, who can be fantastic and frustrating. Joined from Lincoln last season and the Ghanaian reached double-figures in the goal charts.

STOCKPORT COUNTY JASON TAYLOR

The powerful midfielder signed for County on a permanent deal at the start of last season following a successful loan spell during the previous campaign. The 20-year-old played more than 40 games in season 2006-07.

WREXHAM CHRIS LLEWELLYN
The Norwich City youth product first joined Wrexham in 2003 and is now in his second spell with the club having rejoined from Hartlepool in 2005. Llewellyn is a full international for Wales and the energetic striker leads the line well for The Red Dragons.

WYCOMBE WANDERERS JERMAINE EASTER
Easter impressed during Wycombe's League Cup run last season, scoring in every round in which they played, including the semi-final against Chelsea. Gained his first cap for Wales against Northern Ireland last February.

SHOOT ANNUAL 2008 – QUIZ ANSWERS

PAGE 20-21

KNOW YOUR FOOTBALL

10 Questions On... The Champions League Final

1. Filippo Inzaghi
2. Marseille
3. Jose Mourinho
4. Real Madrid and Valencia
5. Jens Lehmann
6. Old Trafford
7. Jerzy Dudek
8. Teddy Sheringham
9. Juventus
10. Moscow

Guess Who?

1. David Beckham
2. Peter Crouch
3. Jens Lehmann
4. Wayne Rooney
5. John Terry
6. Carlos Tevez

True Or False

1. False
2. False
3. True
4. True
5. True

In The Box

Box 1: W
Box 2: I
Box 3: W
Box 4: S
Box 5: H
Box 6: P
Box 7: O
Box 8: I
Box 9: C
Box 10: T
Box 11: N
Answer: IPSWICH TOWN

Anagrams

1. Didier Drogba
2. Rio Ferdinand
3. Darren Bent
4. Martin Jol
5. Andy Johnson

The Eyes Have It

1. Wayne Rooney
2. Ashley Cole
3. John Terry
4. Joe Cole
5. Peter Crouch
6. David Beckham

PAGE 32-33

KNOW YOUR FOOTBALL

Getting Shirty

1. Holland
2. Northern Ireland
3. Brazil
4. Germany
5. Belgium
6. Italy
7. Argentina
8. England
9. Spain
10. Ukraine

What Do You Know About Michael Owen?

1. c
2. b
3. b
4. c
5. b

PAGE 38/39

MASCOT MADNESS

1. Grimsby Town

Crossword

Across: 1. Shrews.
2. Scott. 9. Carvalho.
10. Milner. 11. Alex.
12. Harry. 15. Kanu.
18. Nolan. 20. Norwich.
21. Djibril. 22. Crewe.
24. Noel. 25. Kalou.
28. Imps. 30. Arteta.
31. Moss Rose. 32. Croke.
33. Andrew.

Down: 2. Harte.
3. Welsh. 4. Sammy.
5. Tannadice. 6. McCann.
7. Moor. 8. Crouch.
13. Arbeloa. 14.
Ronaldo. 16. Andre.
17. Bruce. 19. Leicester.
21. Duncan. 23. Easter.
25. Keane. 26. Lima.
27. Upson. 29. Moore.

2. Preston North End
3. Birmingham City
4. West Bromwich Albion
5. Hartlepool
6. Fulham
7. Aston Villa
8. Burnley
9. Manchester City
10. Coventry City
11. Blackburn Rovers
12. Manchester United

PAGE 50-51

KNOW YOUR FOOTBALL

Spot The Difference

Face To Face

1. Jamie Carragher
2. Rio Ferdinand
3. John Terry
4. Frank Lampard
5. Wayne Rooney
6. David Beckham

Crossword

Across: 1. Boston.
4. Drogba. 9. Adebola.
10. Micah. 12. Bent.
13. Defoe. 14. Deco.
17. Blades. 19. Alonso.
20. Primus. 22. Fulham.
25. Wise. 26. Evans.
27. Dyer. 31. Dunne.
32. Glazier. 33. N'Gotty.
34. Forest.

Down: 1. Bromby.
2. Spain. 3. Owen.
5. Rams. 6. Ashton.
7. Rovers. 8. Zamora.
11. Chelsea. 15. Adams.
16. Doyle. 18. Larsson.
21. Savage. 22. Finnan.
23. Sweden. 24. Orient.
28. Yorke. 29. West.
30. Mido.